———————— *These are t*

Canon Michael Saward has had a v...
two curacies, was Secretary of Liv...
Church of England Radio and Tele..... ......, vicar of two
West London parishes, for 20 years a member of General Synod,
for 15 years a Church Commissioner and since 1991 he has been
the Treasurer of St Paul's Cathedral. An award-winning journalist, prize-winning hymn-writer, author, preacher and broadcaster,
Canon Saward has been married for 41 years and has four children and five grandchildren.

These are the Facts

MICHAEL SAWARD

'These are the facts as we have received them,
these are the truths that the Christian believes.'

TRIANGLE

First published 1997
Triangle
SPCK
Holy Trinity Church
Marylebone Road
London NW1 4DU

Bible quotations are from:
The Revised English Bible © 1989 Oxford and Cambridge
University Presses.
King James Version (Authorized Version 1611).
The text of the Authorized Version of the Bible is the property of
the Crown in perpetuity.
The Revised Version © 1885.
The Revised Standard Version © 1971 and 1952.
Letters to Young Churches © 1947, Phillips.
The Jerusalem Bible © 1966 by Darton, Longman & Todd Ltd.
William Barclay New Testament © 1968.
Good News Bible published by the Bible Societies/HarperCollins
Publishers Ltd UK © American Bible Society, 1966, 1971, 1976, 1992.

The publisher takes this opportunity to thank those individuals and
organizations who have given us permission to use and adapt material
for this book. Every effort has been made to trace the owners of copyright material, though in a few cases this has proved impossible and
we apologize to any copyright holders whose rights may have been
unwittingly infringed. We trust that in the event of any accidental
infringement, the owners of the material will contact us directly.

British Library Cataloguing in Publication Data

A catalogue record for this book is available from the British Library

ISBN 0-281-05124-0

Typeset by Pioneer Associates, Perthshire
Printed in Great Britain by
Caledonian International, Glasgow

Contents

PART 1: I'VE STARTED, SO I'LL FINISH

1   Mind How You Go!   3
2   Hooked on Religion?   8
3   Know What I Mean?   13
4   Top of the Pops   18
5   In the Beginning   23
6   Cruelty and Coitus   28

PART 2: GOD'S TRUTH

7   God Almighty!   35
8   That's the Spirit   41
9   Look! No Man   45
10 You Want Problems?   51

PART 3: IT'S THAT MAN AGAIN!

11 God Save the King   59
12 Stories to Remember   64
13 Loaded with Lolly   70
14 Serve You Right   75
15 Pig in the Middle   79

16 Light Dawns   83

17 What's He Up To?   86

PART 4: WHAT'S IN IT FOR ME, THEN?

18 It's Me, Folks   93

19 The Dirtiest Word of All   98

20 Back to Basics   103

21 OHMS   108

PART 5: HEADING FOR THE CHEQUERED FLAG

22 A Hell of a Way to Go   115

23 Dust to Dust   121

24 Are You . . . ?   125

These Are the Facts   129

References   130

*With
grateful thanks to
my secretary,
Rosemary Nicoll,
who typed and retyped and
corrected this book
without a single grumble,
and to Felicity Stockdale,
who, on behalf of the publisher,
took it apart and helped
me to put it together again!*

To the many thousands, from all over the world,
who listened patiently to one, some, or many of
these words and ideas in
St Paul's Cathedral between 1991 and 1996 and
especially to the unexpectedly large
number who, after the experience, asked for
copies or tapes.

PART 1

I've Started, so I'll Finish

1 Mind How You Go!

I wonder what kind of a mind you have? No, I don't mean to enquire whether you are a clever person or not. Some people have the kind of mind that is as hard as nails; others' are as soft as butter. Some people's minds are as gentle as a lamb; others' are as tough as old boots.

Virtually all of us gradually acquire a particular shape to our thinking, almost without our knowing it. The shape of some people's thinking is, however, totally shapeless. Their minds are incoherent and all their attitudes a confused jumble of ideas. What a contrast to those whose minds are set in concrete, whose opinions, once formed, are impervious to every influence. Nothing shifts them, because they have stopped thinking and their reactions are utterly predictable.

Whatever the shape or shapelessness of our thinking, we all have some kind of a 'world view' by which we operate. We may have absorbed it from the culture of the media, politics or religion, but it affects everything we are. Gautama Buddha said, 'The mind is everything: what you think, you become.'[1] History offers us countless examples to illustrate this. Take, for example, the distinct ideas about the relationship between the sexes which have developed. Some cultures are polygamous: men can have a number of wives. A few are based on polyandry: one woman can have more than one husband. Other societies are monogamous: one man and one woman for life. In recent years the West has developed a kind of serial monogamy in

3

which divorce flourishes and one man and one woman stay together for as long as they wish and then separate, probably with new partners. Even more recently there has been a growing pattern of varied, long- or short-term relationships without permanent commitment. I could give more examples; my point is that in most (but not always) cases people's actions are governed by what they *think*.

Take another example, that of religion. The shape of a religion affects people's minds. Buddhism, for instance, teaches that there is no reality. Everything is illusion and at the root of all is human desire. Desire leads to pain and grief, so the great goal is to be free of all desire. My mind must be shaped to follow this, so that I come to Nirvana, where I shall be unmoved by everything and thus free. Such a religion is self-absorbed, focusing on me and my deliverance.

Islam is quite different. For the Muslim, God has fixed everything finally and human beings can do nothing to change it. It is the will of Allah to which people must submit, taking the teaching to others so that they too can accept Allah's will. From the perspective of Islam, all is predestined.

Judaism shapes the mind to accept a carefully codified law, revealed by God. If you keep this law, you will become righteous.

Non-religious philosophies also shape minds. Humanism may take many forms, but the key is that man decides everything since he, or she, is the measure of all. There is only one life, and nothing beyond, so be yourself, and fulfil yourself. That may mean self-sacrifice, or it may mean doing whatever you like. The results may vary, but the mind-set is the same.

For the last two thousand years Christianity has had a basic mind-set. It has varied in detail: Catholic, Orthodox, Anglican, Reformed or Independent. Even so, it has had a unified core to it.

4

God, the eternal creator of all, has come among us, in the person of Jesus, the Messiah. He showed us how a perfect life could be lived, died to cleanse the sin of all who put their trust in him, rose from death and founded a kingdom which will ultimately supersede all human societies. He calls for all humanity to acknowledge him as Lord and Saviour, and he empowers his followers to live according to his will through the Holy Spirit, who is his continuing presence. He will return, to complete his work for all eternity.

That view has radically changed, stemming from the attitudes of rationalist philosophers from France and Germany in the nineteenth century. Thirty years ago an English writer, Harry Blamires, wrote an excellent book called *The Christian Mind*. Right at the start he said, 'There is no longer a Christian mind. It is a commonplace that the mind of the modern man has been secularised . . . it has succumbed to the secular drift with a degree of weakness and nervelessness unmatched in Christian history.'[2] Harry Blamires was certainly not alone in believing this. Today the situation is far worse than even he contemplated. Many people who think of themselves, perhaps vaguely, as 'Christians' have now lost all touch with the 'shape' which has traditionally been recognized as that of the Christian mind.

What has replaced it? A minestrone soup of bits of this, that and the other, drawn from this philosophy, that element of pop-culture, a bit of Hinduism here, a bit of Buddhism there, a smattering of Christianity, a big chunk of superstition, a slice of so-called scientific atheism, a leaven of existentialism, all dressed up in a tolerant sauce of Shirley MacLaine-type New Age 'philosophy'. Add a dash of English indifferentism, American materialism and French cynicism, and your soup of ideas is just the kind of savoury broth that titillates contemporary man and woman and makes little or no demands upon them. If it's new and fashionable, it must be right. As Dean Inge, of St Paul's Cathedral, once acerbically remarked, 'He who marries the spirit of the age will soon find himself a widower.'[3]

Bishop Lesslie Newbigin, one of the ablest Christian minds in Britain in recent years, recently summed up the situation like this: 'There is a danger of knocking out all the fences and becoming part of the pagan stew.'[4]

What is the alternative? St Paul once told the Corinthian Christians that they had 'the mind of Christ'.[5] Elsewhere, he spoke of the need for Christians to 'let God remould your minds from within. Don't', he added, 'let the world around you squeeze you into its own mould.'[6]

Three great twentieth-century minds have advice to offer us. First, James Orr, a great Scottish theologian writing before the First World War, tells us that the New Testament 'comes to man with definite, positive teachings: it claims to be the truth: it bases religion on knowledge ... a strong, stable religious life can be built on no other ground than that of intelligent conviction', not of 'mere feeling', which is the 'vaguest, most unreliable, most unstable of all things'.[7]

Second, the novelist and dramatist Dorothy L. Sayers argues that 'The only really relevant reason to accept Christianity is that you are convinced that it is true.' She describes Christianity as:

The most exciting drama that has ever staggered the imagination of man – and the dogma is the drama. That drama is summarised quite clearly in the Creeds ... and if we think that dull it is either because we have never really read those amazing documents or have recited them so often as to have lost all sense of their meaning. The plot pivots upon a single character and the whole action is the answer to a single, central, problem, 'What do you think of Christ?'[8]

She goes on to say:

> He was not merely a man so good as to be 'like God' – he was God. This is the dogma we find so dull – this terrifying drama of which God is the victim and the hero. If this is dull, then what, in Heaven's name, is worthy to be called exciting?[9]

Finally, Tom Wright, Dean of Lichfield and one of the greatest minds in today's Church of England, gives us this succinct summary: 'The basic shape of Christian theology is creation, covenant, and eschatology – the shape of the creed.'[10]

Here, then, is a real challenge for us. We need to discover 'the Mind of Christ'. St Paul, in his letter to the Philippians, sets out the very heart of the faith.[11] God who becomes man, dies on a cross, is raised and is, for all who believe, the origin, the focus, the meaning and the goal of all things. To submit to him, to allow our minds to be reshaped by him, to know him as Saviour and Lord, gives new meaning to everything, a new sense of purpose and direction, a new dynamic and a new hope. It also offers us the conviction that despite all the Holocausts, the Hiroshimas, the Bosnias, the Rwandas and the countless private and personal betrayals, ultimately God's purpose will triumph over evil. Through faith the Christian mind is shaped and the Christian culture is rebuilt.

This small book is an attempt to put before you the core of the Christian faith. It seeks to give some shape to what it means to be a Christian believer in the changeover years from the second to the third millennium. 'These' (in a nutshell) 'are the facts . . .'.

2 Hooked on Religion?

'Religion,' said Karl Marx, 'is the opium of the people.' 'Man,' he added, 'makes religion, ... it is his self-consciousness and self-awareness as long as he has not found his feet in the universe.' 'So,' he concluded, 'religion is the sigh of the oppressed creature, the sentiment of a heartless world ... the abolition of religion ... is a demand for man's real happiness.'[1]

I am not a Marxist, but I believe that here, quite unwittingly, Marx has hit on something which lies right at the heart of the Christian Faith. Let me try to explain.

Go out into the street with a microphone and a clipboard, and Mr and Mrs Smith – or Mr and Mrs Greenbaum, Mr and Mrs Patel or Mr and Mrs Singh – will all be able to tell you that the world's religions include Hinduism, Buddhism, Judaism, Sikhism, Christianity and Islam. Someone else will tell you about 'The Old Religion', witchcraft, or the Nordic gods, while others will speak of the New Age, the Moonies, the Baha'i faith, and so on.

Many will echo the words of George Bernard Shaw: 'There is only one religion, though there are a hundred versions of it.'[2] To many people that seems obvious. All religions are merely different ways of climbing the mountain to reach God at the top. When I was a boy we used to sing a hymn at my school which included this verse:

Some seek a Father in the heavens above,
some ask a human image to adore,
some crave a Spirit, vast as life and love
within thy mansions we have all, and more;
Gather us in. Gather us in.[3]

If you think in the same way, you will almost certainly look to a future in which we shall all be tolerant of anything that goes by the name 'religion'. You may also argue that we should all try to worship together since, boiled down, we are all worshipping the same God, whatever we may call our religion. Or you may remain agnostic but agree with Arnold Toynbee that 'Religion is a built-in feature of human nature,'[4] a distinctive characteristic of humanity. Every human being, said Toynbee, has a religion, 'even if he denies that he has one, and denies this in good faith'.[5]

What a contrast this is to what you find in the New Testament. There is one very remarkable fact at its heart which very few people notice or grasp. Here, the word 'religion' is almost never mentioned. Nowhere in the New Testament, either in the teachings of Jesus or of his followers, is the Christian community, or its beliefs, described as 'religion'. Whenever the word is used (just three or four times),[6] it refers either to paganism or to (usually) Judaism.

Those early Christians did not believe that Jesus had come to initiate another (new) religion. His claim and his unique acts put him in a different league altogether from every other religious leader. He was no mere prophet. Neither was he a sectarian leader. He was the fulfilment of all God's promises to the Jews, the Messiah, the Christ, the Lamb of God who 'takes away the sin of the world'.[7] Jesus was, astonishingly, God himself. In him God broke into human history in personal form – 'and was made man', as the Creed says.[8] Jesus marked the end of the Jewish monarchy and the

9

Jewish religious system, symbolized by the Temple in Jerusalem and all its sacrifices; he was the promised Servant whose death and resurrection announced a new world. He was the fulfilment of the terrible words pronounced by God through the fiery prophet Amos, 750 years before: I hate your religious festivals. I can't stand them! When you bring me your animal-sacrifices, your burnt offerings, your grain offerings, I won't accept them. I don't want your noisy songs. What I want is justice and righteousness.[9]

Toynbee, Shaw and Karl Marx were all right in one respect: religion – any religion – is humanity's attempt to come to terms with reality. We invent rituals, structure systems and create prayers, all to help us to cope with our feeling of impotence in the face of life's harsh realities. We sense a central reality, a creating God, and we know that we are not worthy of that God. So we try to climb upwards to that perfect focus. We try to make our rituals perfect in every detail, to say exactly the right prayers, to live a faultless life. We try to be good enough. The prophets of all religions urge us to be more religious, more exact, more moral, more perfect; to keep the law; fulfil our religious duties; free ourselves from every desire and avoid all that is taboo or forbidden.

Toynbee was right when he said that all humanity is inherently religious. Shaw's acknowledgement that there are thousands of ways to express this fundamental religious need was also correct. Marx was right too: religion is like a soporific drug, in that it helps to keep human beings sane in all their pain, suffering, and impotence. (However, Marx also claimed that true happiness can be found only when religion has been abolished.)

It was to people with just such an understanding of religion that Paul, in Athens, set out to offer real hope: 'What you worship, in ignorance, I now proclaim to

10

you.'[10] Humanity, said Paul, was looking for God, feeling about to find him, not realizing that he had come among them, had died and risen from the dead.

The apostle John quotes Jesus as calling himself 'the Way.'[11] His death was the final sacrifice for all human sin. God had come to all humanity, whatever they called themselves, whatever their religious practices, race, culture or gender. In coming he was breaking down every man-made barrier, opening the way for all to meet him. And his name was Jesus, which means 'Saviour'. He was the Lord of all creation. To seek forgiveness, people had to trust him. To find the source of true holiness, they had to accept his righteousness as a gift, not strive to achieve an inadequate self-righteousness. To be at one with those of other tribes, other skin-colours, other classes, they had to be baptized into his new family: those whom he was adopting, those who would allow themselves to be reborn by his Spirit.

Search the teaching of Jesus from top to bottom. Search the New Testament high and low. You won't find the creation of a new religion. What you will find is an invitation to all, every man, woman and child, to let God transform them. He will take them in all their disobedience, inadequacy and sin and make new people from them. 'If anyone is in Christ, he is a new creation.'[12]

That was the message. That was the offer. And what we human beings did was either reject it, as the Jews did; turn it back into a religion of ritual and merit, as the pagans did; try to absorb it, as the Hindus did; try to ignore it, as the Buddhists did, or invent an alternative, as the Muslims did.

However, in every age since the time of Christ, there have been those who have accepted Jesus as the unique entering-in of God into humanity. Such people have experienced the new life, new hope, new fellowship and new joy that comes when the Spirit does his

11

transforming work. As the centuries roll by and the world's geography shrinks, men, women and children of every colour, class and nationality have dispensed with religion and found Christ.

In 1953 a film was released on the life of Martin Luther.[13] At one crucial point, a friend, a senior monk, takes Luther to see an event full of religious ritual, relics and almost superstitious devotion. 'What would you put in the place of all this?' he asks. Luther gives his answer in two words: 'Jesus Christ.' Not 'religion', of whatever name. Jesus came to get people off the drug called 'religion'. Think about it.

3   Know What I Mean?

Some years ago I was lunching at the Houses of Parliament with a famous Member. He is a Christian man, indeed he is renowned for his Christian stance on many of the ethical issues which have been highlighted in the past 30 years or more. He had invited me quite explicitly to pick my brains on one particular matter in which I had some experience. As we talked over lunch, it began to dawn on me that, for all his Christian commitment, this man had very little understanding of the Christian faith as the New Testament presents it. It came as quite a shock to realize that he seemed to have a lot of good will but no more than the vaguest kind of humanistic moral sense. He lacked any understanding of God's grace and had virtually no assurance that Christ had died to be his Saviour.

This man treated the Bible as a pious book of universal statements about ethics. He had never discovered any shape or coherence to it: for him it was just a rag-bag of sayings from which to pick and choose. He believed in a two-tier Church in which the religious professionals – bishops and clergy, monks and nuns – had to try to reach high standards of behaviour, while ordinary Christians muddled along as best they could. He was kind, well-meaning and hopelessly clueless. I wondered what on earth Peter, Paul and the other New Testament writers would have made of a man so totally unaware of the teaching which they had carefully

13

handed down in their Gospels and letters. They might have been even more stunned, perhaps, by his complete lack of concern for his overwhelming ignorance.

He was a nice man, a kind man, but, I wondered, did he know God? I'm still not sure. Now, please understand, I am not trying to pillory this famous man. What saddens me is how typical he is of so many people who sit in our churches. He is trying to be a good person, but he is completely confused.

One of the most famous Psalms[1] is widely known by its Latin name, *Deus Misereatur*. It is very brief, only seven verses long, but it contains some really powerful ideas. Six times it calls on all humanity to praise God, to be glad and joyful, and to honour him. And why? Because of three divine characteristics:

1 he has provided justice,
2 he has provided food,
3 he has provided guidance.

The Psalmist was no fool. He knew perfectly well that the world was full of injustice, ignorance and hunger, but he did not make the common mistake of blaming God for them. He knew that most of humanity's woes and griefs were man-made, so he didn't blame God for the problems. Instead he thanked God for having provided, as the Genesis creation stories describe, a world that is fruitful and for having taught us how to arrange our affairs justly and wisely.

He then goes on to ask for God's mercy and kindness in order that human beings – all human beings – might discover the two most important facts of all: God's will and God's salvation. This may seem a tall order – just how are we going to do this?

That is exactly what the Bible is all about. It tells of a God who sets out to open our eyes and our hearts to his nature and purposes. It shows how he repeatedly made these things known, so that when he finally came among us, that coming had been foretold and its purpose explained. The great central themes of the Old Testament present God as holy, loving, and, above all, as unique. The great central themes of the New Testament build on them and reinterpret them, focusing on the living reality of Jesus, the one who, while truly man, was also uniquely God in our midst. That same Jesus revealed in a vivid yet cryptic manner God's will and God's salvation, and actually brought them among us by his death and resurrection.

Jesus did not, and does not, leave it there. Salvation is a pearl of great price, which a human being must prize above all else. It is found by entering a narrow gate and comes to those who openly acknowledge their need of it. Nobody drifts into possessing salvation. You cannot buy it, or merit it; you can only receive it as a gift. You must come on your knees, regretful of all your foolish efforts to deserve it, of all your failures to meet God's demands upon you, of the self-centredness of your motivations and your countless attempts at self-justification. It is a gift available only to sinners. Those who claim to be righteous, or rely on their best efforts to be good enough for God, remain outside the gate in outer darkness, the willing victims of death.

'Yes, all right,' you say. 'You've made your point. I'm just an ordinary person, but like your famous friend I am confused by the Bible. It does seem to be a vast shapeless mass of stories, histories, laws, poems, prophecies and so on. How on earth can you expect me to find my way through that maze?'

That is a fair point. In the last 150 years many scholars have stressed the diversity of the Bible. This has been an important feature of this period of the Church's life. But others, throughout the past 2000 years, have drawn our attention to the great uniting themes which pervade the Bible. How can you get that overview?

A few years ago I stood on top of Mount Diablo, near San Francisco. It stands on its own and it's a long climb. Fortunately I had outside help, in the form of a car and a map and a road, so it took about half an hour to get to the top. Once you get there you have a magnificent view all around. The roads, rivers, lakes and towns fall into place – you can see how they interconnect. Down on the ground below you can see only the bits nearby. Up on the top you see the big picture.

That is possible with the Bible, too. We have books, cassettes and videos from great Christian teachers to be the car, the map and the road. They help us to find the way.

Dr James Packer, a theology professor in Vancouver, offers us such help. In his best-selling book *Knowing God*, he says, 'Paul's letter to Rome is the high peak of Scripture. Luther called it "the clearest gospel of all". Calvin said, "If you understand it, you have a sure road opened to understanding the whole of Scripture." William Tyndale, who first translated the New Testament from Greek into English, called it "the most pure Gospel – the light and way to all Scripture".' Packer adds: 'When the message of Romans gets into a man's heart there is no telling what may happen.'[2] Reading Romans transformed St Augustine, Martin Luther and John Wesley. They became new men.

So, if you want the overview, read and study that letter to the Romans. I have lectured through part or all of it six times in my ministry and it has shaped all my thinking about God's will and God's salvation. It has been my biblical Mount Diablo.

Let's go back to Psalm 67. It explained, as you will remember, the Psalmist's hope for humanity: 'That the whole world may know God's will and God's salvation.'[3]

If you want a Mount Diablo, so that you can see the bigger picture, read Romans. You will never be the same again once you have grasped the message of that letter. Try it – again, and again, and again – but make sure you use a modern Bible: that way it will be a great read!

4 Top of the Pops

The Bible is still the number one best-seller and has been for centuries past. If God were to get the royalties, the sums in the heavenly bank account would be staggering.

What do you make of the Bible? The cynical (most of whom have never read it) dismiss it. Well, they would, wouldn't they? It calls for a radical change of life and the cynical don't want that. Even so, they acknowledge and recognize it as the great foundation document of the Christian faith. This understanding of the Bible has never been seriously disputed by Orthodox, Catholic or Evangelical Christians, however much they may debate its consequences and how it relates to the varying traditions and interpretations which have divided the many churches.

When passages from the Bible are read in the Church of England, they are described in words carefully chosen by the Church. 'This,' we say of both the Old and New Testament readings, 'is the word of the Lord'[1] and we gave thanks to God for them. We acknowledge them to be just that, not simply some ancient human document (though they are that too). Through these words, God is speaking today as he did to our forefathers two millennia ago and more. When we read from one of the Gospels, we describe it as Christ's good news: 'the gospel of Christ'.[2] In this way, the church recognizes the implicit activity of God. We do not give the Gospel our authority. We bow to its own intrinsic authority, as Scripture given by God to instruct and edify his people. Sometimes a New Testament reading makes this claim for its Old Testament antecedents. 'All ancient scriptures,' said St Paul of the Law, Prophets, and Writings (i.e. the Old Testament), 'were written for our instruction.' In a similar letter, in words ascribed to him, he speaks of all scripture as 'inspired by', or 'breathed out from', God.[3] He adds the four purposes for which it has been given to the Christian Church: first, 'to teach the truth'; second, 'to rebuke error'; third, 'to correct faults', and fourth, 'to give instruction in right living'.[4]

In these phrases the Bible is seen in both its positive and negative aspects. It is there to give shape to Christian belief, defining what is true, and to warn us against what is false and to be rejected. It has a similar role concerning ethical behaviour. It warns us against behaviour that is not compatible with Christian discipleship and encourages us to exhibit those characteristics which make both us, and the Church, more Christ-like. Professor William Barclay, famous throughout the world in this last half-century for the many books he has written and for his biblical knowledge as professor of Divinity and Biblical Criticism in the University of Glasgow, summed the passage up in these memorable words:

> . . . all theories, all theologies, all ethics, are to be tested against the Bible. If they contradict the teaching of the Bible, they are to be refused. It is our duty to use our minds and to set them adventuring: but the test must ever be agreement with the teaching of Jesus Christ, as the Scriptures present it to us.[5]

Barclay was a Scottish Presbyterian – but what about English Christians? Do they agree? In the 1980s, the Church of England's House of Bishops endorsed a statement called 'The Nature of Christian Belief'.

Commenting on the Church's conviction that 'the Faith' is 'uniquely revealed in the holy Scriptures', they declared that the Bible's authority is 'paramount for all Christians'.[6] It is, they said, 'the inspired record and interpretation of God's love, at work to liberate and transform our humanity and the world in which we live. We need,' they added, 'this authoritative testimony to set us on the right path.'[7] They coupled both Old and New Testaments, which, they declared, 'must always have a controlling authority',[8] adding: 'we need to place ourselves continually under the Scriptures'.[9] These powerful words from the House of Bishops are the most recent statement of the Church of England's desire to remain under the controlling authority of Scripture.

Sadly, we cannot leave it there. According to the Church Press,[10] only 15 per cent of regular churchgoers have read the Bible, although many, of course, dip into this bit or that bit. No one would pretend that it is an easy book, but the sad fact is that the vast majority of Christians are willing to express opinions about the Bible when they have made little attempt to grapple with it. This is even more true of those who don't pretend to be Christians. I get quite weary of listening to people who have almost no idea of what is in the Bible dogmatizing about it. They use words like 'myth' and 'legend', but they wouldn't know a myth or a legend if they saw one. They parrot phrases they have picked up from the media and think they are being clever, when they are merely exhibiting their ignorance.

Stop and think. These last 60 years have seen more translations of the Bible published than ever before. In Africa, Asia and Latin America, men and women are gobbling up the Bible, and its truth, like hungry people in a famine. It speaks to them and they are nourished. Not so in Europe, where, surrounded by every kind of aid to understanding, even Christians can't be bothered to give any time to the Bible. They sit in front of interminable soap operas for hours and hours every week, but they don't have even an hour a week for the Bible. Is it surprising that ignorance of the Bible among European Christians is so widespread and so destructive of the Christian Church?

What are the consequences of this ignorance? Countless people sitting in churches on Sundays can't tell their Amos from their Ezra, their Mark from their Hebrews, and don't feel an ounce of guilt or shame about it. They can't explain Christian doctrine (the truth of biblical theology) and they don't know how to meet the challenges of an apathetic world with regard to the ethical issues of the day. They are easy prey to the New Agers, the cults, the post-modernists and the lust-and-lottery society which dominates our media. If the Christian inheritance of Europe collapses, and it could do in a generation, it will do so because so-called Christians refused to learn their faith and how to defend it, before it was too late.

As a young man, I grew up in a home where we never went to church, never read the Bible, but thought we knew enough to call ourselves 'Christians'. When, as a teenager, I came to faith, I started to read the Bible daily. It was a slog, but I kept at it and, in my early twenties, I also wrote a page of comment on the passage for the day. Recently, I looked back at what I had written. There were 576 pages in all – nothing very profound, but those comments laid a foundation on which I have built for nearly 50 years. Every word and every page was written before I became a clergyman.

As well as reading the Old Testament once, and the New Testament three times in earlier years, I read and commented on Mark, Luke, Acts, Romans, 1 Corinthians, Galatians, Ephesians, Philippians, Colossians, Hebrews, 1 Peter, 2 Peter and, from the Old Testament, Jeremiah, Lamentations, Ezra, Nehemiah, Nahum, Habakkuk, Ezekiel, Joel, Obadiah, Micah, Zephaniah,

21

Haggai, 1 Chronicles, 2 Chronicles, parts of Isaiah, Psalms, Proverbs and Kings. I say this not to boast, but simply to indicate that it is perfectly possible to do this and to gain great value from it.

This, then, is the challenge to us today. For four hundred years after the Bible became widely available through printing, our forefathers and mothers read it. They soaked themselves in it, many of them, and they shaped much of our history. They gave the Bible time. They gave it effort. They studied it carefully. They became 'the people of the book'. Andrew Jackson said, of the USA, that the Bible was 'the rock on which our republic rests'.[11] Abraham Lincoln called it 'the best gift God has given to man'.[12] John Wesley cried, 'Give me that book, at any price, give me that book of God.'[13] J. R. Green, the historian of the English, said that Bible reading 'changed the whole temper of the nation – a new moral and religious impulse spread through every class'.[14] Reading the Bible can do this. It has done it before. At the Coronation the sovereign is given the Bible with the words, 'Here is wisdom. This is the royal law. These are the lively oracles of God.' I used the same words not long ago when I blessed the Lord Mayor of London on the steps of St Paul's Cathedral and gave him a Bible to mark the beginning of his mayoralty.

Anyone who wants to understand and follow the Christian faith reads the Bible. Don't plan to start doing so next week. Start today!

5 In the Beginning

Was it a Big Bang? And, if not, how did the universe come into being? Some say it was all a matter of chance, others that it was a six-day job in 4004 BC. A few think they can pin down the exact time creation began to nine o'clock in the morning on such-and-such a day. Well, this must surely be wrong if God is a gentleman: no gentleman would consider doing anything even half as strenuous at such an uncivilized hour!

Let's set aside the idea that the creation was no more than a series of accidents, merely blind chance. It takes more credulity than any amount of faith that God exists to believe that the development of every speck of matter was a 100-million-million-to-one shot. It is inconceivable that the human eye just happened. I won't buy that one. Nor will many able scholars who acknowledge a Creator.

So what can I buy? There seem to be three options available to Christians, in all of which a creating God must, in some way, feature. A literal interpretation of Genesis[1] is a matter of absolute necessity to fundamentalists, who maintain that 'the Bible says so'. Now, I happen to regard the Bible as God-inspired and reliable, but I am not a literalist. There are two problems with fundamentalist literalism. First, it makes the big assumption that everything written in the Bible has to be interpreted in a literal way. Why? I grew up on *The Wind in the Willows* and I have Mole, Rat, Badger, Toad, the River Bank, and the Wild Wood in my bloodstream. It's a great story and I believe that Kenneth Grahame meant it to be read, first as a story, and second as a parable of English life in Edwardian times.[2] Mole and his friends were decent English yeomen, Toad was a decadent aristocrat, the Stoats and Weasels were Socialists and Marxists who came out of the Wild Wood to seize power, and so on. The decent chaps would ultimately succeed in chucking them out but from then on they would have to take over from the cocksure foolish Toads. Only thus could civilization be saved and secured for the future.

This is a perfectly feasible interpretation of Grahame's delightful book, which is well argued by his biographer. It isn't a question of 'believing' or 'denying' the story – it's simply a matter of interpreting the document.

Second, a literal reading of Genesis produces one impossibility. Light, as human beings perceive it (day as distinct from night) depends on the existence of the sun – no sun, no light. But, a literal reading tells us that there was light on Day One but no sun till Day Four. So I don't buy the fundamentalist dogma about creation.

Explanation number two says: 'God was the creator but he did it in stages, by means of evolution.' Each 'day' was a great epoch of time. On the face of it, this seems a more thoughtful handling of the time factor and the development of species. I was once persuaded that it might be a legitimate way of interpreting the evidence. But it won't do. Why? Because, like the fundamentalist view, it still leaves us with the 'light on Day One' and 'sun on Day Four' problem.

Think again. Think laterally, not literally, and forget the idea of seven consecutive days. Suppose God chose to reveal the wonderful fact of creation in the form of a great hymn, a liturgical sequence with regular, repeated cadences. It would be entirely natural to find 'And God said', 'let there be', 'God made', 'so it was',

24

'it was good', 'evening came and morning came',[3] and so on. Such 'responses' are the 'stuff' of liturgies.

Now let's pursue the idea further. In the Bible, seven is the symbolic number for completion, fulfilment. Therefore, God describes the completion of his work as a seven-fold sequence. First he reveals the development of his three great sequences or spheres of activity in three 'days', symbolizing epochs of time.

The first sphere is the great divide between 'light' and 'darkness'. Call that Day One. The second sphere divided 'water' from 'sky' (Day Two). Third and last came the divide between 'land' and 'sea' and 'inanimate nature' (Day Three). The three spheres of activity are in place, ready for God's next task.

Then comes the work of inhabiting these spheres. Day Four introduces us to the sun, moon and stars, who rule the Day One sphere. Next, on Day Five, fish and birds arrive to populate the Day Two sphere of water and sky. All is now ready for the climax of Day Six, on which God provides land creatures for the Day Three sphere, whose culminating figure is the human race. The crowning glory has come into being.

To round things off, Day Seven is dedicated to the Creator himself, whose initiatory acts are complete. There is good in all that he has made and he now pauses to take stock and rest, in symbolic statement of the fulfilment of his holy purposes.

That, of course, is not the only biblical creation account. The second version[4] could hardly be more different. In the first, God acts in sequence, with man appearing as the culmination. In the second, humanity, male and female, comes smartly on to the scene. The man has an important and God-given role. He names the living creatures, and God sets him in a garden to cultivate and manage it. He is thus related to the earth and its inhabitants. Even so, something is missing – no, not 'something' but 'someone'. Thus woman becomes man's 'other half', and he knows her to be absolutely right for him. They become 'one flesh',[5] a phrase that evidently means sexual union, in which, nakedly together, they feel no shame.

The two accounts, in such contrasting literary styles, provide one important clue as to their distinct and separate purposes. The first account deals with procreation, fertility and the populating of the spheres – 'Be fruitful and multiply.'[6] The second says nothing about procreation but everything about monogamous union. It can certainly be argued that the second account is more primitive in style and quite probably older than the first.

If that is the case, it makes sense for the earlier tradition to be about the oneness of man and woman, whose sexual bonding is the great foundational human act. On this reading, the later account, which is far more cerebral and lofty, tells us that the purpose of the union was the procreation and growth of humanity, whose fertility populates the earth.

Incidentally, such an interpretation has enormously important consequences. First, it decisively banishes the idea that the Fall (in Genesis Chapter 3) is somehow caused by the discovery of sex. People who take that view completely ignore the meaning of Genesis 2. Second, it introduces the possibility of separating the control of fertility from sexual union. That this discovery took millennia is not the point. 'Family planning' is entirely consistent with a full sexual union. Those who reject it do so because it frustrates God's wish for unrestricted fertility, maintaining that, as medieval theology prescribes, the first 'cause' of matrimony is 'the procreation of children'.[7] The continuing conflict between the Roman Catholic Church and most other Christians hinges on this very point. If union is the key idea, contraception is possible. If, in contrast, procreation is the prime reason for marriage, both logically and morally contraception is not right, since it would deliberately frustrate God's plan. Isn't it interesting how two different views of the creation narratives can cause such radically contrasting attitudes in the contemporary world?

But we must return to the fundamental question. Are the Genesis accounts tenable and, if so, in what way? I have argued that the literalist view is not tenable and that the attempt to tie in God and evolution also falls short. A liturgical structure whereby the three spheres are created and populated in three epochs, the task of creation being fulfilled and rounded off by the resting on Day Seven and its associated 'holiness', is a thoroughly legitimate interpretation; it acknowledges the creation, in sequence, of order and purpose in the universe, and especially in our world, by God. Such an understanding is in no way in conflict with scientific discovery on the one hand, or a divine Creator on the other. It diminishes neither Scripture nor the natural sciences.

Genesis is not a literal description. Nevertheless, it cannot be lightly dismissed as mere legend. It is a great creation hymn to the One who is before, behind, beneath and beyond all. What is more (and most important of all) it makes sense and it draws out the worship of our hearts in love and praise. And, if you don't agree, it's up to you to provide a better explanation.

6 *Cruelty and Coitus*

One of the basic rules of our modern, so-called civilized world is the assumption that if you want to make a blockbuster film, a successful novel or television series, you had better be sure to include one or both of the essential ingredients: sex and violence, butchery and bonking, cruelty and coitus.

If you are tempted to be high-minded and dismiss this idea, let me ask you a question: which parts of the Old Testament come first to your mind? My guess is that most people will remember David and Goliath, David and Bathsheba and Samson and Delilah, for example. People remember stories, especially the stories about what men and women do to each other and with each other.

In Genesis, Cain and Abel are remembered because one killed the other. Joseph is recalled because his brothers put him in a pit and sold him into slavery, and also because his employer's wife made a pass at him and, when he declined, had him thrown into prison. Genesis has its fair share of rapes and murders. Exodus vividly describes the drowning of the Egyptian army in the Red Sea. Later books tell of local tribes who were massacred in what, today, we call 'ethnic cleansing'.

As to sex, there's plenty of that in the Bible. What about that luscious, erotic poem called 'The Song of Songs'? This is not only full of references to legs, thighs, breasts and so on, but includes a handful of coded allusions (common in Middle-Eastern writing)

28

to sexual intercourse. It leaves little doubt about the pleasures of loving and bonking there! Sadly, nearly 30 years ago, an Archbishop of Canterbury (Geoffrey Fisher) told the Press that he regretted that The Song of Solomon had been included in the Bible.[1] It was far too erotic for him. It was not just a love song!

Not long ago, I was talking to a vicar's wife, who told me that her elderly mother had preferred the Old Testament to the New Testament because, as she put it, 'There are more dirty bits in it.' How sad that she had equated sex with dirt.

Try reading the account of the vivid conflict between the teenage shepherd David and the enormous Goliath.[2] It is quite unforgettable. It is also unquestionably violent. Incidentally, in case you are tempted to write it off as no more than a Disney-type legend, perhaps you should know that human skeletons 3 metres (10 feet) tall – the height mentioned in Samuel's account – have been dug up in Israel. We are probably reading fact, not fiction, and the killing of the great soldier by a boy with a catapult has been stored deep in everyone's memory bank, as has David's later seduction of Bathsheba and the arranged murder of her husband.[3]

The plain fact is that most of the really memorable bits of the Old Testament do come into the sex and violence category. Certainly some (perhaps most) people get no further than that. Others prefer to forget the gory bits, or the sexy bits, and concentrate on the noble characters who emerge: Abraham, Moses, Elijah, Solomon, Isaiah, Daniel and so on. Such people are often unable to cope with the down side of their heroes. I recall using a minicab some years ago with a Pakistani driver. He had a Bible on his front seat. 'Are you a Christian?' I asked. 'No,' he said, 'I am a Muslim. But I have a problem with this Bible.' I waited for him to mention some great theological issue, but no. 'I cannot understand,' he said. 'We honour the Prophet Lot.

But in this Bible he behaves disgracefully. He offers his virgin daughters to an evil mob. Then later he has sex with both of them. How can this Bible be true? Our prophet could not be such an evil man.'

My Muslim friend was offended. Vainly I tried to explain that most of the great figures of the Old Testament were painted as real men, flesh and blood, warts and all. Lot was only a minor character. The driver wanted perfect heroes or none at all, however. 'This Bible cannot be true,' he said and that ended our journey.

I believe that he was wrong, and so was the lady who enjoyed the Old Testament for the so-called 'dirty bits'. Those who know the Old Testament chiefly because of its vivid depictions of sex and violence are also wrong. Wrong, I hasten to add, not because these elements should not be present, but because they are, however memorable, not the essential elements in the biblical record. Their job is to tell you that this collection of books, with their histories, laws, prophecies, poems and love-songs, is about real people and real events that happened over a period of nearly two thousand years. They were real people: nomads, settlers, farmers, warriors, lovers, parents, adulterers, murderers, kings, priests and prophets; real people, who laughed, squabbled, cried, fought, lusted, hated and killed. Underneath it all, they were a people who believed, passionately, that they had been called and chosen by the One High God, creator and upholder of all things, to be his people, his messengers to a rebellious pagan world, among whom they were a mere drop in the ocean of humanity.

Now, at last, we're getting to the real core of the Old Testament. Take the word 'testament' itself: it means 'covenant' and 'covenant' means 'promise'.

Those 39 books of the Old Testament are the revelation by God, recorded by men (and possibly some women), of two great promises. One was a promise to

30

Abraham. It was called an 'eternal' Covenant, never to be withdrawn, whereby God, in an act of free grace, mercy or generosity (call it what you will) promised Abraham and his descendants that they would forever be his own special people, and that the whole world would be blessed by them.[4] What does that mean? Most of the rest of this book will try to explain it.

The second Covenant was made centuries later with Moses and the Jewish nation at Mount Sinai, after their escape (or exodus) from slavery in Egypt.[5] This promise was not called 'everlasting' or 'eternal', but it was a promise to the nation. Surrounded with laws, this Covenant also introduced a priestly system of sacrifice.

The New Testament is careful to distinguish these two Covenants. That with Moses and the Jewish nation is called 'obsolete'[6] because Jesus Christ had in his own person fulfilled it and brought it to an end by his sacrifice on the cross. (The subsequent destruction of the Jewish Temple in Jerusalem and the end of the sacrificial system was seen as God's endorsement in history of what Christ had achieved on the cross, where he integrated the New Covenant in his blood, to which he referred at the Last Supper.) The writers of the New Testament did not regard the earlier 'eternal' Covenant made with Abraham as ever having ended. On the contrary, they saw Christians as the true heirs and descendants of Abraham who trusted in God's grace and not in their own obedience to the law. St Paul explains this in at least two of his letters, to the Galatians and the Romans.

Grasp this fact and it will entirely transform your understanding of the Old Testament and, indeed, of the New Testament as well. Instead of an assortment of stories, most memorable for their elements of sex and violence, plus poems, wise sayings, and laws about everything from shellfish to menstruation, and so on, you will discover the record of a timeless promise made by God and how it was fulfilled. The story will take you through the successes and failures of the recipients of God's promise, to its fulfilment in a man called Jesus and will show you how Christ's followers, the heirs of that same eternal promise, point the way to the great and eternal kingdom for which God's people daily pray 'your kingdom come' in the Lord's Prayer.

Enjoy reading your Bible, both Old and New Testaments. Then remember its purpose and its promises, and trust in the God who revealed them to us.

PART 2

God's truth

7 *God Almighty!*

I'm sure that at some time in your life you must have asked the question, 'What is God like?' It is quite likely that you have some kind of picture of God in your mind, but some people, as has been said, 'have a God-shaped blank in the consciousness'.

Human beings have always needed to have some kind of image to fill that blank. The more primitive create idols out of wood or stone, but, as Tolstoy put it, 'When a savage ceases to believe in his wooden God, that doesn't mean that there is no God, but only that the true God isn't made of wood.'[1]

But there are other kinds of image; images in the mind. Some forms of Hinduism imagine the divine being like the infinity of the ocean into which we, as minute drops, are absorbed. Mediaeval man saw God as a regal potentate, before whom ordinary people crawled in fear of their lives. In the Christian tradition many people have a picture of an old man with a great beard, as William Blake,[2] or Michelangelo before him,[3] portrayed him. This is the image of the patriarchal Father, the Old Man in the Sky.

If you were a Jew, or a Muslim, you would want to distance yourself from these pictures. In the same tradition, John Calvin, the great reformer, said: 'We must hold it as a fixed principle that as often as any form is assigned to God, his glory is corrupted by an impious lie.'[4]

This tradition, common to the Bible and the Koran,

maintains that 'no man has seen God at any time.' You'll find that in the Prologue to John's Gospel.[5] For centuries this attitude dominated Christian thinking. No artist would have dared to try to paint a picture of God, for that would have been regarded as blasphemy. Only as Greek pagan ideas crept into the Church did such attempts to represent God become slowly (and after the so-called Iconoclastic controversy) acceptable. Centuries later, the Puritans took the same view. It wasn't motivated by a dislike of art, but by their belief that Jews, Muslims and Christians, as monotheists, were forbidden to create images (actual or cerebral) of what God is like. That is unquestionably the Bible's stance. You can't see God and you mustn't attempt to create an image of him, even in your mind!

How, then, are we to provide any meaning to that little word 'God'? First and foremost, we can know that he is. He is before, beyond, above and within all things, ceaselessly sustaining, upholding and creatively loving the universe that he has brought into being. He is beyond our comprehension, beyond the outer reaches of our finite minds, a pulsating, life-giving focus of mystery. If the reality of God were small enough to be grasped it would not be great enough to be adored.

The Christian who wants to identify with the biblical heritage can use descriptive language, as long as he acknowledges that this will offer no more than vague analogies. For example, God may be described as light, dazzling, effulgent, blazing with cosmic and super-cosmic energy. The prophets, like Ezekiel,[6] and the seers, like the Apostle John,[7] used such language. They used natural imagery – storm, lightning, thrones, crystal, precious stones – but only as a means of hinting at the indescribable. They used cloud and fire as symbols of God's mysterious nature, but none of them thought that God was actually limited, contained or even focused in such ideas.

36

Their purpose was to portray God as *beyond* – awesome, blinding, holy, radiant – and to remind human beings that we are utterly insignificant, no more than moral pygmies in the face of such shattering perfection. Again and again, when men had a visionary experience of God, they were driven to their knees, utterly humbled. Moses, Isaiah, Jeremiah, Ezekiel, John and Paul, all were shattered and drained of any idea of self-worth. 'I fell at his feet as though I were dead.'[8]

God, in short, is not a comfortable, cuddly figure. We may have been made in his image, but we are terribly tainted and reduced by our self-assertion and our fallenness.

Yet, amazingly, the message which comes to each of us through the Bible is: 'Don't be afraid. I am the first and the last. I was dead and now I am alive for ever more.'[9]

This is the unique understanding which Jesus Christ has brought to us. While it is eternally true that 'No one has ever seen God', it is also true that 'God's only Son, who is nearest to the Father's heart has made him known.'[10] That last phrase means that 'he has given us a full and detailed exposition of what God is like.'

So, to grasp what God is like we must study the Bible's portrayal of the man Jesus of Nazareth and learn from him what meaning we are to give to the very word 'God'. Through Jesus we can look beyond the imagery of storm, cloud, fire, light and so on to come face to face with one who is unique in his origin, his conception, his life, his power, his death, his conquest of death, his reigning glory, his presence through his Spirit and his ultimate purpose.

In Jesus, God has revealed his glorious splendour by a unique birth, life and death, a unique victory over the grave and a unique and ongoing presence through the living Spirit. And yet, in all this, God remains one. He does not share his glory, but he reveals himself in three personal dimensions as Father, Son and Spirit – three in one. He is not three Gods, he is one God, known in three ways. This great truth of the Trinity has its expression in both Old and New Testaments.

The image of God is stunning to those who have eyes to see it. Do you remember Elizabeth Barrett Browning's vivid phrase about Moses' vision of God at the burning bush?

> Earth's crammed with heaven,
> and every common bush afire with God,
> but only he who sees, takes off his shoes.[11]

What should be our response to such a God, three in one? The Bible presents three great acclamations of heavenly worship:

> Holy, holy, holy, is God the sovereign Lord of all, who was, and is, and is to come.[12]

> You are worthy O Lord our God to receive glory and honour, and power, because you created all things; by your will they were created and have their being.[13]

> The Lamb who was killed is worthy to receive power, wealth, wisdom and strength, honour, glory and praise.[14]

I tried to convey something of this response to God in a hymn which I wrote nearly 20 years ago on a French hillside overlooking the Mediterranean. I wanted to capture the amazing way in which God takes our tongues of 'earthbound clay' and lights them 'with flaming fire' as we worship our holy God, Father, Son and Spirit.

> O Trinity, O Trinity,
>   the uncreated One;
> O Unity, O Unity,
>   of Father, Spirit, Son:

you are without beginning,
your life is never-ending,
    and though our tongues are earthbound clay,
    light them with flaming fire today.

O Majesty, O Majesty,
    the Father of our race;
O Mystery, O Mystery,
    we cannot see your face:
your justice is unswerving,
your love is overpowering,
    and though . . .

O Virgin-born, O Virgin-born,
    of humankind the least;
O Victim torn, O Victim torn,
    both spotless lamb and priest:
you died and rose victorious,
you reign above all-glorious;
    and though . . .

O Wind of God, O Wind of God,
    invigorate the dead;
O Fire of God, O Fire of God,
    your burning radiance spread:
your fruit our lives renewing,
your gifts, the Church transforming;
    and though . . .

O Trinity, O Trinity,
    the uncreated One;
O Unity, O Unity,
    of Father, Spirit, Son:
you are without beginning,
your life is never-ending;
    and though . . .

May I encourage you not to try to picture God as Father or Patriarch or whatever? Avoid imagining an old man or a king and concentrate instead on God's love and glory. If you need to know what he is like, look at Jesus, for it is only through him that we can approach the All-Holy. 'No one', he said, 'comes to the Father except by me.'[15]

So, when you come to God, you come on your knees. You come face to face with a man on a cross, who reveals God and his glory to you. It's humbling, it's demanding, but it's the real thing.

8 *That's the Spirit*

If Christians were to reinvent the Nicene Creed today,
my guess is that many of them (and especially those
who identify themselves with words like 'renewal' or
'charismatic') would, almost without thinking, start the
third section with the words 'We believe in the Holy
Spirit, the Lord, the giver of *power*'. To support this
theory, we have Graham Kendrick's hymn 'We Believe',
which asserts that 'we believe he sends his Spirit on his
church with gifts of power.'[1]

Power. Our generation is obsessed with it. Some
people long for political power. Some want economic
power. Most want sexual power. Many Christians long
for spiritual power. And they're not alone. Humanity
has always yearned for power. Many of the ancient
world's religious rituals and incantations were aimed at
getting and using power. Gain power and other people
will respect you, listen to you, obey you and fear you.
Some Christians merrily sing 'I'm building a people of
power,' putting into Christ's mouth words he never
spoke.

One power-hungry figure pops up briefly in the New
Testament. He was a Samaritan, Simon by name, and
he had gained quite a reputation with his magic. Luke
tells us that this Simon made 'large claims for himself'[2]
so that everyone, high and low, listened to him. They
called him 'The Great Power' because, says Luke, they
were 'captivated by his magic'.[3] Not surprisingly, Simon
was intrigued by the arrival of the apostles Peter and

John. 'Give me the same power,'[4] he pleaded and tried to buy it. Peter gave him short shrift. 'To hell with you and your money,'[5] he retorted.

The temptation is real enough. We always tell ourselves that if only we had the power we could use it to God's glory. Sadly, it rarely works like that. 'Power tends to corrupt,' wrote Lord Acton to Mandell Creighton, Bishop of London, and he went on to say that 'absolute power corrupts absolutely.'[6] He did no more than recognize the lessons of history. Human beings want to run things, to control things, to manipulate things, to change things. Try reading Machiavelli's *The Prince*,[7] which is the most famous and notorious book on the subject of gaining and using power. It is a ruthless, cynical and largely accurate description of how to behave if you want power and have no scruples about exploiting it.

In recent years the bookshops (especially in the United States) have been full of 'how to' books offering '42 ways' to achieve success in the boardroom, the bedroom, in Congress or even in the Church. All of them are, at root, about power.

Jesus, in contrast, said very little about power. He was concerned about love, service and sacrifice. True, he promised his followers power at Pentecost, but it is interesting that Paul did not speak of power as one of the fruits of the Spirit. It was, instead, a by-product of the Spirit's presence. Even Jesus's promise before Pentecost is an assurance that his disciples would bear faithful witness wherever they went. Nowhere does the New Testament offer encouragement to people who long to say, 'Look at me. I've got power.'

The early Christian Church undoubtedly got it right. The most important aspect of the work of the Holy Spirit was as the personal life-giving force in the universe. It is 'the Spirit', says the great second-century theologian, Irenaeus, who 'sustains all'.[8] His contemporary, the apologist Athenagoras, refers to the Spirit twice as 'an effluence' (and once as the 'ray of the sun' and 'light from fire').[9] Throughout the whole of the second century there is hardly a reference to the Spirit linked with 'power' in any Christian writing.

So why did the earliest Christians stress the Spirit as the 'life-giver'? It all begins in the Genesis story of creation, where the Spirit is likened to a great bird brooding, as life, ordered life, comes forth from the shapeless, formless chaos. It is the Spirit who is God's agent in the bringing of light, order and life.

Such an understanding has powerful implications. If every form of life owes its very existence to God's Spirit, we human beings are, inevitably, charged with neither creating, nor destroying, life thoughtlessly or carelessly. In our world that certainly has consequences in the field of sex and genetics, of family planning and abortion. While the Bible never absolutely forbids the taking of life, we, today, are required to ask ourselves searching questions about the essential God-given value of all life. Such questions inevitably cover the taking of life as a punishment, for food and by abortion. In Christian eyes, taking life is never an easy option and, above all, it is never a casual act.

To acknowledge the Spirit as the unique life-giver has other consequences. All humanity is thereby gifted by God's Spirit. The creative brilliance of a genius, the outpouring of art, of music, of craftsmanship of every kind, is a sign that the Spirit works throughout humanity. God's gifting is in no way limited to those who acknowledge him, believe in him and place their hope in him. That is the measure of his generosity. Some of humanity's greatest achievers have been far from being men or women of faith. Would to God they had been, but they weren't. Yet the Christian understanding remains that their talents were not innately 'natural' to them, but God-given. That is why, in the Creed, we ascribe to the Spirit the life force which is in all creation. All gifts are God's gifts and we human beings are stewards, answerable for their use or abuse.

To many modern Christians such an idea comes as a great surprise. They have come to assume that the Day of Pentecost[11] was in some way 'the coming of the Spirit', who, to put it crudely, hadn't been around before then and who now burst on the scene distributing a collection of goodies like Santa Claus. Not so! Sadly, some who take this view may assume, all too foolishly, that God is interested only in a small range of tuppenny-coloured excitements like 'speaking in tongues', 'exorcizing demons', 'producing miracles' and so on. To such Christians, the Spirit is perceived to be all about ecstatic spontaneity, noise, excitement and a lot of rolling in the aisles. To them it comes as a great surprise to learn that both Scripture and tradition have recognized the Spirit as the one who brings order out of chaos and promotes continuity and the development of holiness of life for both the individual and the Church.

Pentecost brought the fulfilment of prophetic promises to the infant Church. The Spirit was understood in a fresh and very personal way and not just as an 'influence'. The Spirit was not an 'it', but the living presence of Jesus, no longer seen in an earthly body. The infant Church needed that assurance and unmistakably received it. It was the Spirit who expelled Jesus's followers from their insecurity in Jerusalem and gave them real confidence to proclaim the words and work of God.

You and I can tap into that same life-giving spiritual dynamic today and we shall do it best when we declare with heart and soul that, like our forefathers in the faith, 'We believe in the Holy Spirit, the Lord, the giver of life.'[12]

9   Look! No Man

It is no secret that virgins do not get pregnant unaided. Throughout virtually all of human history there was only one way that a virgin became pregnant and you certainly don't need me to tell you how! Today, at least in theory, artificial insemination can cause a pregnancy without actual intercourse but, however it happens, you don't get pregnant without some tangoing between Mr Sperm and Ms Ovum. Although our ancestors may not always have been scientifically knowledgeable, from time immemorial, human beings have known this basic fact of life. If a young woman, any young woman, claims to be both pregnant and a virgin, she is most unlikely to find people credulous enough to believe her. 'Oh yes?' we say, with just the right degree of scepticism to leave her in little doubt that we reckon she's lying – which, as we know, and she knows, she is.

So, when at Christmas-time we cheerfully sing: 'The Virgin Mary had a baby boy, and they say that his name was Jesus',[1] are we fools, liars or just players in a children's fantasy? Do we really think it's true? Are we that naive?

In recent years, more than one bishop and even, perhaps, one archbishop have suggested that it's merely a pleasant story and one which intelligent Christians jettison. I beg to differ.

There are four grounds on which, it is argued, the Christmas story should be rejected:

1 It is merely a legend. Other religions have similar stories.

2 Such miracles don't happen – God is surely consistent in keeping the rules of his creation.

3 The gospel-writers got it wrong. Only two of them mention the Nativity story and either they were mistaken and misled, or they made it up.

4 Faith doesn't need historical facts for its foundation – we should still be Christians even if Jesus had never been born.

What can be said to counter these charges?

First, the scholar Gresham Machen long ago examined all the known suggested parallels and, after 60 pages of descriptions, concluded that there wasn't a single true parallel between the Nativity account and pagan stories.[2]

Second, the 'anti-miracle' charge is based on an unwillingness to accept any supernatural idea. It has been interesting to see the way in which many scientists have accepted the idea of 'random mutation' in the evolution of species. These 'mutations' are unrepeatable 'one-offs'. I find it intriguing that an 'unrepeatable one-off' is seemingly acceptable if you call it a random mutation, but not if you call it a miracle. The anti-miracle charge is no more than a denial of God's reality. The real problem has always been a theological one – 'how could God become man?' – rather than a biological one – 'how did he do it?'

Third, if the evangelists, Matthew and Luke, got it wrong, where did they get the story from and why did they include it? Ultimately Luke's story can only have come from Mary herself. Was she lying? Was Joseph the father or was it some other man? Was it all a cover-up?

What is particularly interesting here is that the two Nativity accounts are clearly quite independent of each other. Matthew writes from Joseph's angle.[3] He, engaged to Mary, is naturally highly suspicious but comes to accept the virgin conception as true and goes through with the marriage. Luke's account[4] is told from Mary's side and indicates her horror and at the same time her realistic recognition that she remains a virgin. Both accounts include divine intervention in quite different ways and many weeks apart. The two accounts don't tie up tidily.

Why include such material if it wasn't true? It is essential to recognize that it wasn't part of the Jewish expectation that the coming Messiah should be born of a virgin mother. The only Old Testament reference is to 'a young woman'[5] and in Hebrew the word does not necessarily mean 'virgin'. Centuries after Isaiah, the Septuagint Greek translation from Egypt uses the explicit word 'virgin' and Matthew uses it in that form.[6] Luke never mentions it. He was writing for Greeks and a reference to a virgin birth, if it wasn't true, would not help but hinder the acceptance of his Gospel. The Greeks were used to stories of gods seducing women and Luke would clearly want to distance the conception of Jesus from such fables. Neither Matthew nor Luke could expect the story to help either Jews or Greeks come to faith. The only advantage to be gained depended on its authenticity and, if the story was correct, they couldn't properly omit it.

Incidentally, although Matthew and Luke are the only Gospel writers explicitly to mention Jesus's conception, John hints at the story when he mentions that the Jews implied that Jesus was 'illegitimate'. Clearly, some of the Jews knew, or believed, that Mary had conceived out of wedlock. John, perhaps the closest of all the disciples to both Jesus and his mother, makes no attempt to hide the discreditable accusation.[7]

Matthew and Luke, therefore, identify the time, place and family of both Mary and Joseph, independently, accept that the accounts are factual and present them as such. Christianity has always rested on historical fact. Times, dates, places, families, kings, emperors, all are mentioned to make the physical and temporal location clear. The Christian faith is not myth- or legend-based; it is neither a cyclic fertility religion, a mere philosophy nor a moral code. For example, at its very heart, in its Creed, it makes specific reference to Pontius Pilate and in the birth narratives, to Augustus Caesar and Herod the Great, actual historical figures. 'This actually happened' is what the Christian writers assert.

Furthermore, the story of the virgin conception remains consistent in the Christian tradition from Luke and Matthew onward. It is found in our earliest primitive Creed[8] and in the writings of Ignatius, Bishop of Antioch, the city to which Paul and Matthew's Gospel are most closely linked. Ignatius wrote only 20 years after John's death. There is no gradual development of this doctrine of the virgin conception.

Listen to these phrases from Ignatius, taken from three of his letters. He speaks of Jesus as: 'born, yet unbegotten, God incarnate . . . sprung from Mary'[9] and elsewhere: 'Jesus . . . was conceived of Mary . . . sprung from the seed of David and from the Holy Spirit.'[10] Again, most explicitly, he reminds his readers that: 'You are absolutely convinced that on the human side he was actually sprung from David's line, Son of God . . . actually born of a virgin.'[11] These words were written by a man steeped in the traditions of Matthew and Paul. The virgin conception continued to be a recognizable feature of the Christian gospel, asserted by Justin Martyr and Irenaeus, in their apology and defence of the Christian faith. John, Ignatius, Justin and Irenaeus are each a generation apart, no more.

There were, of course, attacks on the idea of the virgin conception. Those Jews who didn't become Christians not surprisingly rejected it. The pagans rejected it. The Gnostics, who were a brand of pseudo-Christians, rejected it. But the Christians stood by it and the vast majority still do. We declare it in our creeds. It is an unbroken tradition, based on reliable texts (and not just one doubtful translation).

The doctrine has, however, given rise to two confusing additions which are not contained in the Bible. One is the teaching that Mary remained 'ever-virgin'. There is no evidence for this in the Bible. The idea is rooted in the fear of sex, even marital sex, which came out of Greek paganism and gained acceptance in the Christian Church in later years. The second addition is the consequential belief in the immaculate conception of Mary in *her* mother's womb. Protestant Christians reject these ideas, as do many Anglicans and Orthodox Christians. In culpable ignorance, some people (especially journalists) speak as if the Immaculate Conception and the Virgin Birth refer to the same event. The former legendary one refers to the birth of Mary, the latter credal one to the birth of Jesus, a generation later. It is quite possible to believe in Jesus's virgin birth without accepting any 'immaculate conception' or 'perpetual virginity'. Some would argue that such beliefs have actively damaged and undermined the essential doctrine of the Virgin Birth as a result.

You may wonder why a virgin birth is important. Does it matter? The New Testament is marked by a strong doctrine of the divine nature of the Word who was made flesh. Jesus is spoken of as the essence of God, who existed before all things, the exact likeness of God, the eternal Word, without sin. How could that eternal being, in whom the full divine nature existed from eternity, become human? That was the question. It still is.

One answer (soon rejected) was what might be called the 'additive' idea, according to which Jesus, a normal child, was at some point in his life 'added to' – endowed with the element of divinity. It is not clear

49

when this happened – in the womb, at birth, at baptism? Christian Scientists still hold this idea, but it won't do. It is a heresy called 'Adoptionism'.

The best explanation I have ever heard came from the Greek Orthodox Bishop, Kallistos Ware. I heard him preach in our Cathedral not so long ago. 'Jesus,' he says, 'was unique. Truly man but not only man.' He adds, 'No new person began in Mary's womb. The preexistent Son came in human form.' Jesus was, says Ware, 'begotten *outside time* from the Father, without a mother. He was begotten *in time* from his mother, without a father.'[12]

This is the historic Christian doctrine. It takes us far beyond materialistic 'How did it happen?' questions and places at the core of our belief the coming together of God and man for our salvation, one who was without sin, yet fully human, into our world.

That is the reason why the angels sang, why the shepherds worshipped, why Mary and Joseph believed, and why our Creed[13] asserts it. The Virgin Mary did have a baby boy 'and they say that his name was Jesus.' And that's the truth.

10   You Want Problems?

I find myself fascinated by the things which some people regard as obstacles to faith. Someone will come up to me and say, 'I'm not a Christian because I can't believe in the resurrection' or 'I can't believe in miracles' or 'I can't accept the virgin birth.' They are surprised when I don't react. They are even more surprised when I say, 'Miracles, virgin birth, resurrection – they're no problem to me.' I can see them thinking, 'Is this man stupid or what? He must find it hard to swallow such crazy ideas.'

Then I play my ace. 'You want something that takes a bit of believing?' I ask. 'I'll give you three problems. If you can handle those, then miracles of a physical, bodily kind are a pushover.'

Problem One is a philosophical problem. 'How can the infinite become finite? Surely that's an impossibility?' I follow this with Problem Two: 'How can the eternal become temporal?' (That's a theological problem.) Perhaps hardest of all is Problem Three: 'How can righteousness become sin?' (A moral problem.)

These three questions lie at the very centre of the Christian faith. If I wanted to lie awake at night puzzling over Christianity, it would be those questions which would cause me concern. After all, if God can become man, if the creator of eternity can become a baby at a point in time and space, and utter perfection and holiness can be made to be sin on the cross, mere physical puzzles, such as how Jesus could be born of a

51

virgin mother, perform miracles and rise from the dead, fall easily into place. Such facts are totally consistent with the greater picture.

Let's look briefly at the first two problems and more carefully at the third. How can the infinite become finite? How can the eternal become temporal? In short, how can God become man? That, more than anything, is the sticking point for Jews and Muslims. To them, the idea that God could somehow enter into humanity is utterly unacceptable. God is one, full stop. What intrigues and perplexes them is the extraordinary fact that Christians also believe that God is one. All three religions are adamant that there is only one God. To Jews and Muslims it is inconceivable that the oneness of God can somehow be developed, extended, broadened into the doctrine of the Trinity: one God, yet three 'personae' within that oneness. Why do Christians not settle for 'one is one and all alone and evermore shall be so?'

The shortest possible answer is that all the first Christians were Jews and therefore monotheists, firm believers in one God. Everything about their upbringing, culture and religion was founded on this. Jesus transformed everything they knew about God. Everything that they had been taught about the unique nature of God seemed to be exhibited in Jesus who was there, standing among them and, when he left them the reality of the Spirit was the same. Father, Son and Spirit were, amazingly, all the same God. What they experienced of the one was true of the others. As they wrestled with this shattering idea they realized that the symbolic heart of the Temple, the Holy of Holies, was a perfect cube,[1] which described the living presence of God: one entity, yet three equal dimensions. The apostle John saw that same three-in-oneness in his great vision of the heavenly city.[2] Thus Jesus's followers understood that God had revealed himself as Father, Son and Spirit, three, yet

52

one. Jews and Muslims have never come to terms with this idea, but it is at the very core of Christianity, just as the Holy of Holies was at the core of Judaism and the heavenly city is at the core of the Christian's ultimate hope. In the Holy of Holies, infinity becomes finite, the eternal becomes temporal and righteousness becomes sin.

It's the third of those which is surely the hardest of all to grasp. God is, by definition, 'holy' or he is nothing. Man knows that he, by contrast, is 'sinful', a creature that falls short of his Creator's purpose. I know that I am not perfect. I know that, face to face with God, I should be agonizingly aware of the searing holiness which would burn and destroy me, for I could not confront it. That was the experience of the prophets of old: they fell on their faces in awe and horror.[3] They didn't smile and say, 'Hi, Lord'. They were utterly shattered. The holiness of God appalled them, opened their eyes, their hearts and their consciences and drew from them the cry, 'Go away, I am unclean.'[4] It is that terrible sense of God's holiness which modern men and women (including many Christians) have lost. No one comes to terms with the meaning and plan of Jesus until he has his eyes opened to see the blazing and painful fact that God is holy and he is a sinner. When the hymn-writer wrote, of Isaiah's vision, 'Bright the vision that delighted once the sight of Judah's seer; sweet the countless tongues united to entrance the prophet's ear,'[5] he was appallingly distorting the biblical words. Isaiah was horrified and fell on his face. The vision was anything but 'sweet' and he was neither 'delighted' nor 'entranced'.

In his second letter to the Christians in Corinth, St Paul sets out the terrifying idea in all its stark awfulness when he writes that Christ 'was made to be sin for us, who knew no sin; that we might be made the righteousness of God in him'.[6]

53

One recent Bible commentator says of these words, 'There is no sentence more profound in the whole of Scripture . . . here is the gospel of reconciliation in all its mystery and all its wonder.'[7]

The impossible happened. On the cross Christ 'bore our sin'.[8] The apostle Peter describes Jesus as 'the righteous for the unrighteous that he might bring us to God'.[9] The unbelievable, the morally implausible, happened.

And, surprise, surprise, the Jewish rituals had for centuries prefigured it. Ritual cleansing and ritual forgiveness had required the death of a lamb without blemish. The worshipper brought his lamb to the priest in the Temple, laid his hands on its head[10] and the lamb was killed and its blood offered as the price of forgiveness. How vital, how essential, was that sign of laying hands on the lamb's head. By so doing, the worshipper identified his sinfulness with the sinless lamb and transferred his sin and guilt to the sinless, yet sin-bearing lamb. When the apostles said, 'he bore our sins' and 'he was made to be sin for us who knew no sin', they were recognizing that what the Temple had seen daily in ritual, was now, once and for all, happening in total reality, on the cross. Righteousness, the divine righteousness of Jesus, was taking upon itself all humanity's moral filth, moral sewage, and suffering the unspeakable agony of its consequences.

So, says St Paul:

this is the ground of your hope. This is the means of your cleansing, this is the divine method of declaring you are forgiven. Accept it, I implore you, accept it as God's greatest of all gifts. Receive this good news and pass it on to others. You were under God's judgment upon sin. Now you are accepted, forgiven, cleansed and renewed.[11]

Forget the incidental problems of miracles. If God, the infinite, the eternal, the utterly holy, can enter humanity and take upon his shoulders our sins and the just judgement which they deserve, this is the most marvellous news that any human being can ever hear. As in the Jewish rituals of old, I can lay my sins upon Christ and rejoice in the forgiveness which is his gift to me. And I can do it right now.

PART 3

It's that Man Again!

11 God Save the King

We have jumped the gun, however. It is time to go back
a bit and explore something of who and what Jesus, the
baby of Bethlehem, the boy from Nazareth, understood
himself to be. Some kind of a king, perhaps?

Have you noticed how every year, around Christmas,
kings become fashionable? In church after church,
kings are on show. School after school mentions them
and sets up plays about them. Kings throughout history
are a thoroughly mixed lot. Take, for example, King
Wenceslas. We call him 'Good King Wenceslas' and sing
an entirely fanciful carol in which the 'good king' and
his page set out to help a poor man with meat, drink
and pine-logs on the day after Christmas, the Feast of
Stephen. There was indeed a Wenceslas, a young prince,
who was murdered by his pagan brother in or around
930 AD, in Bohemia, but the carol is pure fantasy.

Next on to the scene is King Herod. Because the New
Testament mentions four Herods, many people get them
tangled up. Let's work backwards. Two appear in the
Acts of the Apostles: one, Herod Agrippa the Second,
meets St Paul, who appears on trial before him.[1] His
father, Herod Agrippa the First, has earlier executed
James, brother of the apostle John.[2] In the gospels we
meet Herod Antipas, who agreed to the murder of John
the Baptist.[3] This Herod's father, known as Herod the
Great,[4] had ten wives and fourteen children, and he had
murdered three of his eldest sons and one of his wives.[5]
He is the Herod who, in the last few weeks of his life,

59

dying in horrible agony, sent his soldiers to murder a so-called 'king', born up to two years earlier in Bethlehem. All four of these Herods were kings of a kind, but Herod the Great was the only one of any stature, having reigned for many years and built the great Temple in Jerusalem.

Perhaps foremost of all the kings who are in people's minds at Christmas-time are the 'Three Kings of Orient'. They pop up in carols and hog the limelight in Christmas cards. Riding on camels behind a blazing supernova in the sky, they arrive at a manger in a stable on the night of the birth of a baby Jesus. Named Caspar, Melchior and Balthasar, they ride off home by a back road, their place in history secured. Well, not history, perhaps, for the only facts we know about these figures are in the Bible. The Bible tells us that 'magi [astrologers] came from the East',[6] having seen a star (not, incidentally, a 'bright' one), about two years earlier. They went first to Jerusalem, then to Bethlehem, where they found 'a young child' in a 'house' and gave him gifts of gold, frankincense and myrrh. They weren't kings, there weren't three of them and there was no bright star; nor did they go to the manger on the night of the birth. None of that is in the Bible. It's simply popular legend, which took hundreds of years to develop. Their names, their so-called 'kingship' and much else, are all made up by well-meaning but foolish people. I can never understand why people won't leave the Bible alone to speak for itself.

Now, despite all these kings and pseudo-kings and might-be kings, despite our habit of anticipating the birth in Bethlehem, liturgically by three weeks and commercially by anything up to four months, the biblical readings used in church calendars before Christmas focus on John the Baptist, a strange, wild figure in a rough camel-hair coat, eating wild honey and locusts, who came as a prophesied messenger, to prepare the

Jewish people for a coming Messiah.[7] The key meaning of the word 'Messiah' is that of anointing a king, whose royal duties include giving sight to the blind, hearing to the deaf, preaching good news to the poor, cleansing lepers, helping the lame to walk and so on. These actions are expressly mentioned in various prophetic passages, especially in the writings of Isaiah, so that when, in prison, shortly before his murder at the hands of Antipas, John the Baptist sends his anxious question: 'Are you Jesus, the one we're expecting or is it to be someone else?' Jesus replies, in a kind of code, 'See what I am doing – I'm fulfilling the promised actions of Messiah, the anointed king, to the letter.'[8] His words must have greatly reassured John. He was now certain that Jesus was the Messiah, the anointed king of the Jews.

Many times in the Gospel accounts Jesus explicitly speaks of 'the Kingdom of Heaven' which he has come to inaugurate and which brings peace to those who enter it, but conflicts with the forces of this world who reject its character and purpose.

What are these characteristics of the Kingdom of Heaven? Jesus came 'preaching the Kingdom'[9] and Paul and others saw their role as exactly the same. The Old Testament prophets spell it out very clearly. The coming kingdom has four marks and these are illustrated by one great biblical passage which we read every year at Christmas.[10]

The coming king, who will found the new kingdom, will himself have four qualities, as marks of his kingdom. As 'Wonderful Counsellor' he will proclaim justice. As 'Prince of Peace' he will proclaim peace. As 'Eternal Father' he will proclaim stability and as 'Mighty God' he will proclaim universality. Thus the kingdom will be timeless, eternal, without geographical limitation, open to people all over the world; it will be a community at peace within itself, where injustice will have been banished. As the Messiah, Jesus has come to inaugurate it and, despite the hatred, evil, and suffering which will be directed at him and his followers, he will triumph over death. On his ultimate return, he will finally bring to fruition a kingdom which will completely fulfil his promises and prophecies.

How does Jesus convince us that this is all true? He does it in five ways. First, by the vivid stories he tells, 'parables', as we call them. Each describes some facet of the kingdom. Again and again he says: 'the Kingdom is like . . .' and then he tells his story. Often his disciples cannot grasp the point and he knows that ordinary people certainly will not. In that respect at least, Monty Python's *Life of Brian* got it right. People in the crowd certainly got it wrong, as Jesus said they would. Hearing, they would not hear and, seeing, they would not see.[11] But, secondly, Jesus also teaches quite directly. In the Sermon on the Mount[12] he explains, in what we call 'the Beatitudes',[13] the fundamental characteristics of the Kingdom. It will stand human values on their head. Happiness in the Kingdom comes to the rejected, the lonely, the hungry, the tearful – in short, to all who acknowledge their need of a Saviour and reject the way of self-satisfaction and self-justification. He shows how these ideals relate to the religious practices of his day, overturning and fulfilling them. Third, as we have seen, Jesus's life transforms those of others, healing, liberating and overcoming human need. Fourth, he faces the ultimate test, when his kingship is mocked and rejected as he dies on the cross and yet is triumphant, his task completed. Finally, he rises, returns to his Father, sends his Spirit and promises to return in glory. Christians await this return in continuing expectation that all will ultimately be resolved: evil and injustice will be banished and peace will reign in an eternal community of worldwide believers.

Jesus the Messiah, the anointed King, does not face,

and never has faced, serious competition from all the other kings. We confuse ourselves and others with our sentimental Christmas festivities. He is in a different league altogether. That baby is King of the Universe, Lord of the Galaxies, the one Final Solution to all humanity's problems. Bow your knee and worship him.

12   Stories to Remember

Jesus, as we all know, was a great story-teller. He had the amazing gift of being able to express a tremendous idea, a profound theological truth or a painful moral challenge in a memorable anecdote. But there was a problem, and he was alert to it. People would listen to his stories and remember them for weeks, months, years – even 2000 years – and still not grasp the point. 'Seeing,' he said, 'they won't see, and hearing, they won't hear.'[1] Even his closest friends, his twelve disciples, couldn't understand what he was talking about.

Take, as an example, Jesus's short stories about being lost and found.[2] He tells three stories, all linked, about finding something that has been lost. The first story is very brief. It tells us of a shepherd who has 100 sheep, loses one and searches in the desert until he finds it. He throws a party to celebrate. He has saved just 1 per cent of his possessions, but he's happy.

The second story is about a woman who has lost one silver coin out of the ten she possesses. In today's values, she owns £300 and has lost £30, 10 per cent. She is delighted when she finds the missing coin and throws a party to celebrate. Like the shepherd, she is H-A-P-P-Y! It's a great feeling.

So we come to the third story. This one is much more complicated. We call it 'The Prodigal Son', but the word 'prodigal' wasn't in the English language until the fifteenth or sixteenth century. Shakespeare used it in *Hamlet, Richard II* and *The Merchant of Venice*.[3] It certainly isn't in the King James Bible. By using it, we undoubtedly distort the purpose of the story as Jesus told it, because the story is about three men, not one, and they all play major roles, as we shall see below.

All three stories are about the appropriate response to finding something that has been lost. The message is aimed at those who criticize and sneer at successful evangelism. 'This man Jesus actually seems glad to talk to, and eat with, the world's no-goods,' grumbled the religious professionals, the Pharisees. It is to answer that snide, harsh self-righteousness that Jesus tells the stories and asks, 'Isn't it right for the shepherd and the woman to be pleased when they find lost sheep and lost coins?'[4]

The last story is much harder to accept than the other two. It's about a man who got 50 per cent back. Let's try to unpack the story piece by piece. First, the three men: a father and two sons. The father is generous, self-sacrificing, even foolish. He would normally, like any good Jewish father, one day pass on his property and his possessions to his two sons, but he is put under pressure. 'Dad, I want . . .' says one of the boys and, of course, like all growing youngsters he's got to have it at once because he's one of the *now* generation, the *me* generation, who have never learnt patience and don't care tuppence for next week. 'Dad, I really need . . .'. Dad weakens; he wants to be liked, to be generous, to trust the boys to grow up as mature men. 'OK,' he says, 'let's split it.' Both young men get their share of the money. One holds on to his legacy, puts it into the building society, or some safe, sensible, secure investment and gets on with the daily life of the farm. Son number one is a credit to his family, responsible, a wise and prudent heir. Well done, son number one! Your dad's got every reason to be proud of you. You're a thoroughly reliable, moral and worthy citizen. And because you are, you're also, perhaps without realizing it, a boring, pompous, self-righteous and self-satisfied prig. You've every reason to be proud of your behaviour. You are a real pillar of the community, Mr Morality himself. One day they'll make you a magistrate. You could even become a Member of Parliament and make speeches about moral values. There's nothing wrong with that, as long as you practise what you preach.

Son number two is an altogether different kind of customer. If his elder brother is the epitome of self-righteousness, then he is the supreme example of self-centredness. He is the archetypal existentialist, for 'now' and 'me' are his key ideas. He reminds me of the famous question put to F. E. Smith, Lord Birkenhead, by President Woodrow Wilson. 'What, in your opinion,' asked Wilson, 'is the trend of the modern English undergraduate?' Smith's reply was a classic: 'Mr President, the trend is steadily towards women and drink.'[5] Son number two in our story is just such a hedonistic youth. No way is he going to save or invest his legacy. Quick as a flash he turns it into hard cash and heads for the distant fleshpots, the first-century equivalent of Las Vegas, well away from home. There he sets out to have what the foolish world calls 'a good time'. It was once said by George Villiers, the 2nd Duke of Buckingham, that the Duke of Monmouth lived 'as if the world were made only for him'.[6] Similarly, Edward VIII was said by one of his closest friends, Walter Monckton, to believe in 'a God who dealt him trumps all the time and put no inhibitions on his main desires'[7] – son number two to a T. If you've got it, flaunt it. And he did. Of course, the inevitable happened. The money ran out. His fair-weather friends vanished, as did the gold-digging ladies. He was broke, homeless and very hungry and, to crown it all, there was a famine. No one could or would help him and there were no soup kitchens. Even worse (since he was a Jewish boy) the only casual work available was on a pig farm. Because he was desperate and famished, he took the job. He even envied the pigs their pig-swill and you can't, as a Jewish boy, sink lower than that.

Well, you know the story. After a while, even though he was still hungry, he'd had enough, a metaphorical bellyful. So he set out for home, embarrassed, humbled, ready to accept the disdain and punishment which his father would justifiably pour upon him, the boy who had let the family down and dragged their name in the gutter with his irresponsible behaviour. Son number two had reached the end of the road. He was worried that his family might not even open the doors to him. He decided that his best plan was to beg for a job and apologize for his folly.

I'm sure you remember what happened. Dad welcomed him with open arms, made a tremendous fuss of him and threw a party. 'He's come back from the dead. It's wonderful. Kill the fatted calf!'

Son number one heard the noise and blew a fuse. 'My brother deserves to be flogged, to be hanged, and the old man has lost his marbles,' he fumed. 'He's let him off without even a caution. He isn't even on probation. What is the world coming to? What we need is a bit of law and order!' And off he stormed in a righteous huff.

What was this story of the three men all about? What was Jesus trying to say? I suspect he had two aims. One was to show the Jewish religious hard-liners that the day was coming when there would be a great influx of the hated Gentiles into God's Kingdom and, when that happened, it was to be a cause for rejoicing and not grumbling about their past misbehaviour and pig-keeping habits. The outsiders, who had been as good as dead, were going to come alive, to return to God. Penitent, they would admit their sin, their guilt and their idolatrous and immoral behaviour, and God, the Father of Israel, would welcome his long-lost children and throw a party for them. Needless to say, the religious hard-liners would be shocked at God's behaviour. They would go off into their ghetto and complain that their righteous, moral behaviour made them the rightful recipients of any parties that were going. This is one interpretation of the story and, in my view, a thoroughly acceptable one, but it's not one we very often hear, because most of us understand the story in terms of the individual characters, as Jesus told it.

The story comes home to us more easily in directly personal terms. Jesus needed to get the message across to the world's self-styled goodies, who relied on their own self-righteousness and were very quick to blame the not-so-virtuous. God's arms, like those of the father in the story, were – and are – wide open for those who came to him genuinely acknowledging their failure, stupidity, greed and sin (if you want to use a religious word), and admitting their guilt. Now that's a crucial point. When I retold the story above, I left it out. I wonder if you noticed? I said nothing about the son admitting guilt or sin. I just said that he got fed up and decided to go home, where he'd be better off. But that's not what he did. Instead, he came to his senses and a moral and religious transaction went on in his mind. He didn't come home excusing himself, saying that he couldn't help himself, that it wasn't his fault – he'd been led astray by other people – or, worse still, that it was his father's fault for giving him the money; he should have known better. No, son number two doesn't try to shift the blame. He takes it upon himself, fair and square: 'Father, I have sinned against God, I'm not fit to be called your son.'[8]

Recently, I read a newspaper article about a young woman who had, sad to say, acquired a venereal disease. She complained that it wasn't fair: she certainly wasn't promiscuous. Why, she could count the number of her lovers on the fingers of two hands! Amazing! On her

68

reckoning, the dictionary should define promiscuity as 'more than ten sexual partners'.

God doesn't offer open-armed forgiveness to the self-righteous, even if they are bad and think they're not, let alone to those who are quite good and very sure of it. God offers open-armed forgiveness to those who know that they've got to 'come clean' before him. Of course, I'm using the phrase 'come clean' in a different sense from the usual one. They know they must admit to him that they are coming 'not clean'. They need to acknowledge their failure, inadequacy, sin and guilt.

Inevitably, the implied question of a story like this is 'Which kind of son are you?' This is the question Jesus left with those he addressed. So, which kind of son am I? When I hear the good news that someone who was lost has come to faith, do I want to blame them for what they've been, or identify with them because I know that my story is theirs? I too need that forgiveness, cleansing, new life and new hope. It's available and, even better, it's free! So I face a choice. Will I own up and ask for forgiveness while the offer is open? That's what the story was, and still is, all about.

13   *Loaded with Lolly*

A hundred and fifty years ago this year, Karl Marx, in the introduction to his critique of Hegel's *Philosophy of Right*, coined a phrase which I used at the beginning of this book and which has rung down the intervening century and a half like a great tocsin, an alarm-bell to humanity. 'Religion,' said Marx, 'is the opium of the people.'[1] Strictly speaking, this idea didn't actually begin with Marx, because others, including Charles Kingsley,[2] had expressed a similar view. Religion, they argued, eased the pain of life's injustices, making people docile.

Well, I'm sure that throughout history there has been some truth in this theory and that some people will always, knowingly or unknowingly, let religious ritual, ideas and language dull their brains. A good example is the way in which some people give beauty precedence over truth concerning the language of the Bible and of the liturgy.

Let me explain what I mean. Many times since I was ordained I have heard well-meaning people say that they admire the Sermon on the Mount.[3] 'So full of beautiful ideas,' they enthuse and then look to me to endorse their pious sentiments. They are shocked when I do nothing of the kind. Admire the Sermon on the Mount? I don't! It frightens the life out of me – it's absolute dynamite. It blows all your genteel piety sky-high. Jesus sticks his knife deep into our human pretensions and draws blood. He gets right to the core of our hypocrisies, uncovers our hidden hates, lusts and greeds and leaves no one with even a rag of self-righteousness to cover their spiritual nakedness. He rips apart our delusions about religion, morality, charity and so on, revealing our mixed motives for what they are, and unmasks humanity's constant pretence. He offers us a recipe for true happiness which includes bitter persecution, poverty, pain, sadness, mourning, a nil bank balance, an empty fridge and social exclusion – and that's just the 'Beatitudes'.[4] He digs deep into our desire for revenge, for the sexual manipulation of others, for telling half-truths, condoning divorce and gaining a glowing reputation for generosity, prayerfulness and ascetic piety. He condemns us for blaming others for the very sins we commit, for the ramshackle reputations we build on totally inadequate foundations and for the way in which we all try to have our cake and eat it at the same time. That's the Sermon on the Mount!

We like to hear those great words: 'Blessed are the peacemakers, blessed are the pure in heart', 'Do unto others' and so on. They dull our minds and soothe our brains. They drug us and make us feel good. It is only when you stop and look (as we have just done) at what the Sermon on the Mount is all about that our complacency is smashed and we begin to see why the religious leaders wanted Jesus out of the way. He challenged the soft, saccharine caricature of religion to which people had been accustomed.

It is with all this in mind that we look at another of those devastating stories Jesus told, the one about a rich man and a beggar. There is some evidence that Jesus may have taken over an existing story and given it a new twist. Only Luke passes it down to us;[5] it doesn't appear in any of the other Gospel narratives.

The rich man, who is not named, but is sometimes called 'Dives' because that was the Latin word for 'rich man' used in the Vulgate (the Latin Bible), is, it seems, contentedly living in luxury. Outside his gate is a destitute beggar, just about alive, covered in festering sores. Time passes and both die. Their roles are reversed and now Lazarus is in bliss, which Jesus calls 'Abraham's bosom'. This meant that he was relaxing at Abraham's table, the heavenly feast. The rich man, on the other hand, is outside the gate, excluded, in agony, longing for refreshment and finding none. Being a materialistic, self-centred, bossy character, he expects Lazarus to be at his beck and call. 'Do this. Fetch that. Tell my brothers,' he demands.

But it's too late. His life, says Jesus, was the rich man's proving ground and he blew it. There's no second chance, according to Jesus. He had everything and clung to it. The story doesn't say that he gave even the leftovers to the beggar, only that the beggar hoped for them. Jesus gives the beggar a symbolic name, Lazarus, which means 'God will help.' Clearly no one else would, so he was totally dependent on God and other people. Jesus finishes the story by underlining the great divide. Now, he says, is the time to choose and act. There will be no second chance. Lastly he warns us that no special miracle, no resurrection, will, in itself, change human self-centredness. God offers humanity the choice and the freedom to choose and take the consequences.

Now we come to the meaning, which brings us back to Marx and the opium. Naturally we don't forget the story of Lazarus and the rich man, but – and it's a big but – have you noticed how easily we identify with the hope of ultimate bliss? We're on the side of Jesus, Abraham and Lazarus. We don't identify with the rich man. So it's all right. The baddy gets his come-uppance, justice is done and we can all go home to lunch in peace.

There's that opium again. It dulls the reality. We've missed the point. We are much too comfortable.

We shouldn't be. I calculate that virtually everyone who can afford to read this book, even the poorest among us, is among the top 5 per cent of the world's wealthiest people. The really seriously rich are in the top 0.5 per cent. Even the unemployed in our country are better off than vast numbers of people across the world. We in the West – Europeans, Americans, Australians and even those from Asia and Africa who can travel the world – are the world's rich people. We are Dives. I am and you are. Compared with two-thirds of the world's population, we live in comfort, even in luxury. We do not go hungry. We have never begged in our lives (except perhaps for a bank overdraft). We have access to excellent medical care. We do not go about in rags and no street cur has ever licked festering sores on our bodies.

This story is about us and is told to us by Jesus. Around our world, lying outside our gates, are the millions upon millions of Lazaruses, Mrs Lazaruses and baby Lazaruses. Sometimes they peer at us through our televisions; they are ulcerated, starving and disease-ridden; their water-supplies are polluted, their eyes crawl with flies and they lie waiting for crumbs from our Western stockpiles of food. They wait, and they wait – and they die. Of course we are appalled. Someone should do something. It's terrible. Then we switch off the television, sit down to another steak, down another whisky and continue to live as if they didn't exist.

No, this story is no religious opium. Jesus sticks the knife in and twists it – hard. He gives it an eternal dimension. If that's how you want it, don't squeal when your turn comes. Death will open your eyes if nothing else will. You had it made but you did nothing.

Let's be clear about one thing. This story is not anti-rich and pro-poor as such. Abraham had been a rich man but he was in bliss. Dives was rich and in hell. This story, then, is about what you do with your wealth. There can be hellishly mean and vicious poor people. There can be wonderfully generous and self-sacrificial rich people. No, this story isn't a Marxist story about redistribution, about taking wealth from the rich and handing it to the proletariat.

The message of this story is actually quite simple: assess yourself truly, see yourself in the mirror, then act. God has given you what you have. Now use it! Love your neighbour as yourself. For starters, get out your cheque book, but don't just throw money at the problem of poverty. Give yourself back to God and let him show you what to do with your life, and, while you're at it, smash that opium bottle!

14   *Serve You Right*

Just over 30 years ago Joseph Losey made a film called *The Servant*. It was a great critical success and won acclaim for three of its actors, James Fox, Sarah Miles and Wendy Craig. Most of all, it transformed the film career of Dirk Bogarde, turning him from a well-liked matinée actor into a distinguished star. His portrayal of Barrett, the man-servant to an aristocratic layabout was, said the *Daily Express*'s film critic, 'like being hypnotised by a viper'.[1]

The essential aim of the story was to show the way in which the servant was able to corrupt and destroy his master by a mixture of slimy deference and brooding malevolence. It was a great contrast to the utter loyalty expressed a few years later by Hudson, the butler, in the much-admired *Upstairs, Downstairs* television serial,[2] also seen all over the world. In that role, Gordon Jackson showed how a servant is not to be despised when his approach to his task is based on a concept of duty; Hudson feels honoured by the responsibility placed upon him by the Bellamy family.

One of the most important parts of the Old Testament is the sequence called 'The Servant Songs' of Isaiah. In these four songs, which we find in Isaiah chapters 42, 49, 50 and 53, are some of the most significant prophetic words in the whole of the Bible. They act as a focus for one of the great themes that dominate the whole of the Scriptures and they still speak to us today, 2500 years later.

I want to try to summarize what that ancient prophet was expressing in the hope that you will find it as fascinating – and as radical – as it has been for me in the past 30 years, since I first began to get to grips with it.

First, a mysterious, shadowy figure, called simply 'My servant' is introduced to us. God has chosen him, inspired him and entrusted him with the task of establishing justice on the earth. From his mother's womb he has been called to this task, and prepared for it. He is gentle and kind, but he is also as sharp as an arrow and his words cut like a sword. He has two tasks: to restore the Jewish people and to bring salvation to the Gentile world. This dual role fulfils the covenant-promise made by God to Abraham 1000 years earlier: that the whole world would be blessed through his descendants.[3] Through Isaiah, God once more speaks of his dual purpose for humanity. God, you might say, has long horizons.

There is more to come, however, and the prophecy is tough and uncompromising. This holy figure, this Servant, this redeemer, will be despised and rejected. Though he is gentle and always obedient to God's message of hope, God's good news for the world, the response of humanity will be to flog him, to spit in his face, to rip the hairs out of his beard and reduce him to something hardly recognizable as a man, his moral perfection concealed beneath the effects of the hatred vented upon him. The Servant will suffer the horrors of utter rejection. Even his own people, the Jews, will regard him as God-forsaken, the subject of divine judgement, silent, bowed and bloody. Ultimately, he will be executed with criminals and buried in a rich man's tomb. Even as he dies he will pray for his executioners.

And to what purpose? This Servant, says the prophecy, will be 'wounded for our transgressions, bruised for our iniquities',[4] the bearer of all humanity's sin, though he himself was sinless. All seems utterly lost, yet, ends the prophecy, 'I will give him a place of honour'[5] and triumphant success. He shall see all that he worked for fulfilled in his offspring when they receive his salvation. Faced with such an astounding saga of tragedy and triumph, even the world's rulers will be silenced as they ultimately recognize the vindicated Servant.

What an astonishing prophecy! But who is this Servant? Dr John Goldingay, principal of one of the theological colleges of the Church of England, offers us a solution. In one of the songs the Servant is called 'Israel'.[6] Are the Jewish people themselves 'the Servant'? Their history certainly tells of a people who have stood firm against terrible suffering, culminating in the twentieth-century's Holocaust. In some respects they fulfil the role, but, says Goldingay, 'it doesn't quite fit. In the prophet's view, Israel herself is rebellious, not righteous. She needs the ministry of the Servant . . . before she can function as God's servant.'[7] 'To be the Servant,' he adds, 'is certainly her calling' but 'there is one particular Jew who has lived up to the portrait . . . and that is Jesus of Nazareth.'[8]

Here, then, in these four Servant Songs, is a prophetic testimony to mankind's unique Saviour, the Servant who fulfilled the prophecy in every way. Jesus's preparation for his role began in Mary's womb. A gentle, faithful teacher, whose message was for Jew and Gentile, he nevertheless was, and remains, despised and rejected. He was executed in violent horror, among criminals, yet he prayed 'Father, forgive'[9] as the nails bit into his flesh. No wonder that Jesus's followers, both Jews and Gentiles, have seen the Servant Songs as the greatest prophetic testimony to his role and task.

That is not all, however. As Goldingay puts it, 'While Christians are convinced that Jesus alone met the challenge in the fullest sense, this does not mean that the songs are now a dead thing from the past . . . [They are] still God's vision for his people and his challenge to them'.[10]

That's why the apostle Peter, having learnt the hard way that Jesus, the King and Messiah, was also the Suffering Servant, taught Christians to accept their own role as the people of the Suffering Servant.[11] We have good news for the world, Jewish and Gentile. We are called to live as the Servant did, holy, blameless, a people with a God-given message and mission. We, too, like the Servant, must face scorn and rejection, the sneers of the crowd and the clever. If necessary, we too must accept hostility, violence and undeserved suffering, even death itself. That was the Servant's destiny, to which he was faithful. It may also be ours. Triumph and vindication will come later, as they did for Jesus. We are not called to be successful winners in this life, but faithful Servants, as he was.

What a contrast these Servant Songs offer to Dirk Bogarde's servant, the obnoxious and egregious Barrett. To him, his master was someone to be cheated, corrupted, humiliated and despised. Service was demeaning and to be used to undermine the master, destroying his character and credibility. Barrett lacked all humility.

But what does Jesus offer? 'I am among you,' he said, 'as one who serves.'[12] 'The servant is not greater than his master.'[13] The most crucial of all the titles which the Pope holds, and the hardest for him to express, is that of 'servant of the servants of God'. This is not, however, a private title peculiar to the Pope. It is God's purpose for all Christian people, for his whole Church. We are all called by the faithful, suffering Servant, to be the servants of the servants of God. That is our destiny, our task and, above all, our greatest privilege. There is no greater honour than to be the servant of the servants of God.

15 Pig in the Middle

The middleman is the man most likely to get shot. He is the fellow who takes the risk, the huge risk, of acting as go-between, negotiating terms on which agreement may be reached between two parties. He may be the half-way house in a war, an industrial or political dispute, or even a matrimonial breakdown. He speaks to, and for, both sides, but he is on neither side. He is, to use the technical word, the mediator. He may, in contemporary terms, work for the Conciliation Service, for the United Nations, or for a marriage guidance organization.

He rarely receives medals and may get nothing but hatred. Fifty years ago, a famous Swedish diplomat, Count Folke Bernadotte, worked as a mediator in both World Wars. He was then appointed by the United Nations to act as a mediator in Palestine. In September 1948, Bernadotte was assassinated by Jewish terrorists. He was a good man, who sought a just solution to an impossible conflict. He was willing to take risks and he paid the price. Terry Waite is a more recent example of a mediator who had to pay a terrible price, though, thankfully, he lived to tell the tale.

The sad end of Count Bernadotte is a timely reminder that no nation is without its flaws. Jews, Greeks, British, Germans, Americans, Russians, Japanese, Chinese – none of us are pure and blameless, innocent victims, always in the right, and nor are the others always the baddies. So, too, in politics, economics and marriage, there are almost invariably two sides to every story and the middleman is constantly vulnerable. He will bear the brunt of the conflict.

In the New Testament we find the same idea. 'Jesus,' wrote the author of the letter to the Hebrews, is 'the mediator of a new covenant.'[1]

The word 'mediator' is used only six times in the New Testament and three of those occur in this same Letter to the Hebrews. Jesus is, the writer tells us: 'the mediator of a new covenant', 'the mediator of a new covenant' and 'the mediator of a better covenant'.[2]

The same word is used by St Paul of Jesus in his first letter to Timothy. 'Jesus,' he says, is 'the one mediator between God and humanity'.[3] Twice more he develops the same idea, this time in his letter to the Galatians,[4] where he raises the crucial issue of how Jesus can be a mediator. After all, a mediator is an intermediary, standing between two parties.

We're getting into deep water here. In the Bible a much earlier figure is introduced as a mediator. His name was Moses. He acted for God in bringing his law, his commandments, to the people and also acted as the spokesman, the mediator, on behalf of the people in their dealings with God. It was Moses who came down from Mount Sinai with the stone tablets and who splashed 'the blood of the covenant' on to the Jewish people,[5] thus identifying them, through the principle of sacrifice, with God, who longed to cleanse and forgive them. This instituted a system of daily animal sacrifice in the Jewish Temple, as a potent symbol that the gulf between a loving, yet holy, God and a sinful but chosen people could only be bridged by the shedding of blood. This was a powerful expression of the alienation caused by human sin and the awful price which was required to cleanse and sanctify the people. The system culminated in the annual atonement ritual when the Jewish High

80

Priest alone entered the holiest place in the Temple and offered blood for the sins of his nation.

We find this concept very hard to grasp nowadays. We see death, murder, butchery and genocide all over our world but we do not see any religious sacrificial symbolism in the shedding of blood. To a first-century Jew, however, the blood shed in the Temple was the symbol of hope and cleansing. As the letter to the Hebrews reminds us, 'without the shedding of blood there is no forgiveness.'[6]

It ought not to surprise us, therefore, that the offering of the lamb by the high priest was such a powerful image. The supreme significance of the death of Jesus was its sacrificial element: he was the Lamb of God, offered up for our sins.

So what is the Bible saying to us about sin? It is saying that sin – which is no more than human disobedience, including our refusal to be what we should be and our readiness to think, speak and act in ways contrary to God's declared will for his creation – has created a gulf between a holy God and his soiled and spoiled creatures, which they cannot bridge.

It also declares that the only way in which a loving God can bridge that gulf is to come among us, as one of us, to live a perfect life and be sacrificed as a spotless innocent lamb offered by a sinless priestly mediator. As St Paul says, Jesus is 'the one mediator between God and man, who gave himself as a ransom for all'.[7] On the cross the lamb bears our sins, secures our forgiveness and bridges the unbridgeable gulf. Jesus is therefore the high priest, the sacrificial lamb, and, by offering himself, he acts as the mediator between a holy God and sinful humanity. Mercy and justice meet and love triumphs. Sin is not condoned, but dealt with. God offers cleansing, forgiveness and eternal life to all who will receive it as a free gift. The new covenant or promise has superseded the old. The Temple and its sacrificial system are obsolete, because Christ has offered one final, everlasting sacrifice for sin.

Where does this leave us? In the Old Testament, when a person brought his lamb to the priest to be sacrificed, he had one essential act to perform. If he failed to do it, the offering was ineffective and useless. As he handed the lamb to the priest he had to place his hand on the animal's head.[8] By so doing, he identified himself with the sacrifice and symbolically transferred his sins to the animal. When the lamb died, his sin was obliterated. It was a powerful symbolic act, essential to the ritual.

If Christ is the Lamb, the Priest, the Mediator, as a would-be Christian what must I do? For my sin to be removed, cleansed and forgiven, I must place my hand on the head of Christ and identify with him as he bears my sin on the cross. In the words of St Paul, 'I have been crucified with Christ.'[9] The old me is dead, my sins are forgiven and I am a new being.

Few people realize that their sin has been taken away by Christ on the cross. Yet you can know that same cleansing and forgiveness. Lay your hand on Christ now. Let him be your sin-bearer, your Mediator, your Saviour. 'Behold the Lamb of God, who takes away the sin of the world,'[10] John the Baptist said of Jesus, and that promise is for us. Half a century ago I accepted it, so I know it to be life-changing in its impact.

16 Light Dawns

The English language is full of vivid phrases which capture the dawning of a new idea or perception. We say things like: 'The penny dropped'; 'It all clicked into place'; 'The scales fell from my eyes'; 'Eureka! I've got it'.

All these phrases fit the moment, described by St Luke,[1] when two friends of Jesus were jolted out of their understandably disconsolate and depressed state as they walked the 7-mile road to Emmaus after the crucifixion. The two friends had been talking with genuine puzzlement about the strange rumour they had heard that Jesus wasn't in the tomb. It was being whispered that some of his women followers had seen an angelic vision declaring Jesus to be alive. Could such talk be trusted?

As they walked, they were joined by a stranger who, to their surprise, explained all these events as being the obvious fulfilment of various Old Testament prophecies. At Emmaus, the stranger sat down to eat with them, broke bread and vanished. In a flash they knew who he was!

An hour or two later, having rushed back to Jerusalem in the dark, the two friends met the eleven disciples and gabbled out their news. They heard that others too had seen Jesus and, moments later, there he was, in the room with them. What an amazing evening: depression, joy, fear and excitement, all within a few hours.

Two essential details stand out from the rest. First, the two friends needed the stranger to spell out the meaning of what had happened. Despite all their knowledge of the Old Testament, which they must have heard being read week after week in their local synagogue, and despite the fact that Jesus had told them the purpose of his ministry during the months they had spent with him, the penny still hadn't dropped. It took the symbol of the broken bread to open their eyes.

It is one of the sadder facts of history that although a Jew, Jesus of Nazareth, explained to his fellow Jews that he was their promised Messiah and Suffering Servant, 2000 years later, the penny still hasn't dropped for most Jews. On that first Easter evening Jesus told his followers, 'This is what is written, the Messiah must suffer and must rise from death and in his name the message about repentance and the forgiveness of sin must be preached to all nations, beginning in Jerusalem.'[2]

Some years ago, I heard a Jewish man, who is also a Christian theologian, reminding us Gentile Christians about the universality of the gospel, which is for all humanity, whatever our gender, race or culture. Jesus died and rose for all and, over the centuries the same penny has dropped for people in nations all over the world. Even so, history contains countless examples of Christians like those people on the Emmaus Road. They go to church every week, they read the Bible and hear sermons and still the light hasn't dawned. I was just the same. Jesus's message was explained and explained, yet still I didn't get the point. One of my daughters put it very accurately, when, as a child of four, she said of a preacher, 'I heard him. I didn't listen, I only heard him.' That sums up perfectly the fate of so many preachers.

The friends going to Emmaus had done the same for months or even years and I was just like them. Perhaps you are as well. You may be on a church council or

Synod, sing in a church choir or even be a clergyman. Yes, you could even be a bishop and still the essential meaning eludes you.

E. M. Forster summed up the message of his book *Howards End* in one famous phrase: 'Only connect.'[3] That's just the problem: many people never seem to be able to 'connect' with what it meant for Jesus to come among us, live, die and rise again.

There was another essential element in the story of that road to Emmaus. The friends needed not only words of explanation. They needed (and got) a powerful symbol. Jesus took bread, thanked God for it, broke it and gave it to them. The symbolism was unforgettable. Christians all over the world repeat that action as a powerful means of recalling who Jesus is and what he did. We do it every day in St Paul's Cathedral, where I work and, in doing so, we act as believers have done ever since Jesus's day.

That's why Christians need the Bible and the Sacrament of Holy Communion. We read and we understand. Jesus comes to us and our eyes are opened – the penny drops. That realization has dawned on millions down the centuries, as men, women and children meet Christ in their own Emmaus road.

He walks it every day. Go out and meet him there.

17 What's He Up To?

What exactly is Jesus of Nazareth up to these days? Where is he and what is he doing? And how, if at all, does it affect us, in Hackney, Hamburg or Honolulu?

Those are not flippant questions. I ask them in deadly seriousness. Christians go on celebrating the Ascension of Jesus and St Paul tells us that 'God raised Christ from death and seated him at his right hand in the heavenly world'.[1] So what does that mean?

If you go out into the street and ask people, 'Where is Jesus Christ?' I suspect that most of them will talk about him in the past tense, if at all. He was on earth centuries ago. He was crucified and some say he rose from the dead, but he's long since gone. Most people actually think Jesus is dead, yet all over the world, Christians say the Creed, their statement of belief, which declares: 'he ascended into heaven and is seated at the right hand of the Father. He will come again.'[2]

Orthodox Christian belief acknowledges Christ as seated in glory in heaven in the place of highest honour. Who is to say how literally we should take that idea? What does matter is the fact that he is alive, in the place of highest honour, that he has a continuing task to fulfil and hasn't finished with us yet.

What, then, is he actually doing? In the visionary Book of Revelation John sees him as a priest-king who rules the churches. The Letter to the Hebrews adds that in heaven he intercedes for them.[4] What does this mean?

The Letter to the Hebrews has more to say on this

subject than any other New Testament document. It is steeped in the language of the Jewish Temple in Jerusalem, where, until it was destroyed by the Romans in AD 70, once every year, on the Day of Atonement, the high priest entered into the Holy of Holies – the symbolic presence of God – taking with him the blood of a sacrificed animal, the ritual price of atonement and forgiveness. He offered it to God for his own sins and for the sins of the nation. Year after year it was repeated, an outward ritual only.

However, the writer of the Letter to the Hebrews tells us, echoing the passage in Matthew's Gospel where the curtain concealing the Holy of Holies is torn down at the time of the crucifixion,[5] 'Jesus has entered, not just into a ritual copy, but into the very presence of God.'[6] There, says the writer, 'Christ offered himself, the Lamb of God, a unique, single sacrifice once for all, for our sin, and sat down at God's right hand.'[7] The sacrifice was ended, the work of atonement completed and accepted, and so he reigns, not in the posture of a supplicant but as one whose chief task is over, a seated priest-king. He has acted as our sin-bearer and now he intercedes for us, bringing the Church's prayers, our prayers, to the very ear of God. Because of Jesus's work, the way to God is open, our worship is accepted and our needs are always known to our loving Father.

Sadly, we can't leave it there. Christians of different traditions divide at this point. The controversy seems to hinge, believe it or not, on the translation of the Letter to the Hebrews from Greek into Latin dating from the 390s. Jerome, the translator, twice uses a present tense to translate the aorist tense, which is a past tense implying an action at a point in time. On a third occasion he again uses a present tense to interpret an ambiguity where a past tense would have been more consistent.[8]

'Oh,' you say, 'not Greek and Latin grammar!' Well, it may seem a bore, but when I tell you that with those translations Jerome created one of the great doctrinal divides, first between East and West, and second between the Western Catholic Church and the churches of the Reformation, you may realize how tiny bits of grammar can cause hugely significant differences in church liturgy, especially the Eucharistic liturgies. The divide still exists today, within the Church of England and across the Anglican Communion.

What is the issue at stake? Follow Jerome, as many Christians have, and, in one sense or another, Christ is perceived as still presenting (perhaps even still offering) his sacrifice. Therefore the sacrifice is not in the past but is being continually presented. To those who share this view the Church offers the sacred elements in Communion, so that they may in some way enter into that continuing action.

Those who reject Jerome's present tenses in favour of the Greek aorists' past tenses maintain that Christ's offering was presented and accepted and is now the basis for the Church's worship: the Eucharistic elements are the signs of Christ's death, his completed sacrifice. Now they are not offered to him, but given to us as a sign of unmerited grace.

These different understandings profoundly affect the psychology of the churches, the task of their clergy and the degree of assurance that animates the worshippers. Followers of the Jerome tradition are reluctant to assure Christians that they are saved because they believe that his offering is still continuing to be presented. Those who follow the Reformation tradition, on the other hand, assert that Christians have indeed received assurance of salvation, of which the bread and wine are the visible and tangible signs.

Even the actions of the eucharistic president indicate which view he adopts. What he does with the bread and wine in his hands speaks volumes to those who understand these things. Is he demonstrating an offering made to God or a gift from God to the congregation.

Which view is right? I unhesitatingly support those who reject Jerome's mistranslation. In this I am a Reformation man, following the logic of the Letter to the Hebrews. I believe that the unique sin-offering has been made and accepted and that our task is to receive its symbols with empty hands and full hearts and give ourselves back to God in gratitude. The essential Eucharistic movement is from God to us, not vice versa. That's what grace means. Either way, however, Jesus is not just a historical figure. He is alive and at work, interceding for his people.

Charles Wesley puts it concisely in his great hymn:

> Jesus, the Saviour, he reigns
> the God of truth and love
> when he had purged our stains
> he took his seat above.[9]

In those words Wesley is following John Chrysostom, the great Eastern Father, who said: 'When therefore you hear that Christ is a priest do not think that he is always exercising priesthood: for, once for all, he exercised the priestly function and after that he took his seat.'[10]

In Christian worship we recall that great act. Jesus is not vanished, dead, gone forever. He is in heaven, reigning and, through his Spirit, he is here with us.

What we do, in the service of Holy Communion, hinges on what Jesus has done and is doing. As I've tried to explain, this isn't trivial, just one of those hair-splitting arguments that theologians enjoy. A Jewish rabbi once asked me to explain the two views. When I did so, he could see that it was a matter of great importance.

So, next time you say you believe that Christ is 'seated at the right hand of the Father', pause for a moment and ask yourself, 'What do I mean?' and 'What is he doing?' It could seriously affect your spiritual health.

PART 4

What's in It for Me, Then?

18 It's Me, Folks

Annette Lawson is an academic who has worked in universities in London and California. Her major publication, *Adultery*, is sub-titled *An analysis of love and betrayal*. In it, she attempts to set out one of the major philosophical transformations which has taken place in Britain and North America in the past quarter of a century.

As far as I know, Lawson invented the vivid phrase which describes the new philosophy that has swept the West. She calls it 'the Myth of Me'.[1] It's her way of focusing on Tom Wolfe's earlier phrase, 'the me generation',[2] and she powerfully makes the point that the past 30 years have seen a huge growth in the attitude to life which sets out consciously to discover 'me' and my true potential. The name of Abraham Maslow features prominently in this movement, which is based on the kind of existentialism typified by the writings of Jean-Paul Sartre and Albert Camus. Today, it's all part of the fashion called Post-modernism.

'Yes,' you say, 'that all sounds very clever and it's full of long and flowery words, but what does it mean?' Sartre had a phrase which, though it sounds very cynical and harsh, sums it up well: 'Hell,' he said, 'is other people.'[3] To counteract this, he and his followers invented, or made popular, the idea that the real me can only flourish when I decide what I want to be and do, and then go for it! By doing so I 'authenticate' myself, as the cliché goes. The real me is freed when I give full rein to all that me means.

This kind of idea is tremendously attractive. The ordinary man and woman, faced with philosophers, novelists, playwrights, films and television ads, all telling them: 'Fulfil your potential', is impressed. It's a charter for self-expression and, whether in education, the cinema, politics or personal relationships, the thought that I discover the real me by expressing my own wishes and instincts is hugely appealing. 'Do your own thing' is a seductive philosophy and it has, as a result, swept through the West since the 1960s.

Not surprisingly, some Church leaders have been captured by it. In the 1960s, they fell into line behind the secular prophets endorsing the need for personal integrity. 'This,' they said, 'is *your* truth.' 'That is *my* truth.' 'Find what is true for *you* and go for it.' In California, the most successful prophet is Robert Schuller, who has built his lavish 'Crystal Cathedral' outside Los Angeles on the phrase 'Possibility Thinking'. It perfectly captured the American Dream. Authenticate the real you; be positive; don't worry too much about words like 'sin'; go for what you believe. Down with negatives, up with positive, possibility thinking. Find your true self. It was the perfect recipe for the Myth of Me. Don't hold me back! I'm discovering, expressing and authenticating the true Me. I'm exploring my true potential. Wherever it leads me, I will go. That is how to find real satisfaction in life. It all comes down to spontaneity and my impulses. The 'now' is everything. If I feel it, if I want it, then, to be Me, I must have it. Me, Now and Yes – these are the keys that unlock life's potential.

Annette Lawson opens up this scenario brilliantly in her book and shows how it has led, inexorably, to what she calls 'the flight from commitment'. If hell is, indeed, 'other people', as Sartre said, then to hell with other people! What I want is everything. That's the high road to self-fulfilment, so don't get in my way.

What an amazing contrast all this is to the path which Jesus walked and taught! He said: 'Whoever wants to be first, must be the very last . . .'[4] Whoever causes the little ones [the children, the simple, ordinary person] to stumble and fall' – it would be better if he were pitched into the sea with a millstone round his neck.[5] 'He who wants to follow me, let him deny himself and take up his cross.' 'Let him die to self.'[6] 'Cut off whatever offends – hands, feet, eyes – it's the only way.'[7]

Obviously, we are not faced with a straightforward either/or situation. There are people around who are masochists, pathologically unable to cope without mentally (or even physically) flogging themselves through self-hatred. When Jesus taught his followers to 'love your neighbour as yourself'[8] he was recognizing and endorsing the need for genuine self-love and self-respect, and the desire for self-fulfilment. You cannot love others 'as yourself' if you don't love yourself first.

He said that he had come that people might have life 'in all its fullness'. God did not create the human race so that he could obtain sadistic pleasure from watching its tragedies and waste. He intended men and women to find fulfilment in themselves, and in each other, subject only to their living within the terms of their maker's handbook.

This is where the problem lies. The human-fulfilment people, the Myth of Me people, refuse to accept one vital factor, which the Bible calls 'sin'. That little, three-letter word means putting me at the centre, making Me the arbiter in all things. In short, sin and the Myth of Me are identical. There is simply no way that the Christian faith and the Me Myth can walk hand in hand. They are fundamentally opposed, at the deepest level, because at the heart of the Christian faith are two divine commands: 'Love God with all your heart, soul, mind and strength' and 'Love your neighbour as yourself.'[9]

To love God first means to seek his will and to fulfil it – that's where I get my deepest fulfilment. Then, from that fulfilment, I love my neighbour as myself. At once the Me element falls into place. It isn't ignored or underplayed, but it is disciplined. That Me is made in God's image and likeness and will only find itself when Me truly reflects God's purpose for my life. That's when the sin element loses control of me and it is voluntarily yielded to God. There's no sense of fulfilment to match that. That's what life, real life, is all about and while human beings hold back from that commitment life will never yield the deepest fulfilment. When Jesus was asked to describe the search for such a life, he spoke of a man seeking the perfect pearl which, when he found it, was worth selling everything to obtain.[10]

So what's gone wrong in our Western world? Our forefathers knew that, however much they failed to reach fulfilment, that God is real, true, the source, centre and goal of all satisfaction. Today, most Westerners no longer really believe this. They have fallen for the adman-speak that promises them everything in the name of the Me Myth. In the name of self-fulfilment every commitment – business integrity, marriage, political loyalty – can be broken and dishonoured; nothing is sacred except getting what I want. That's the message at the heart of the Me Myth. It's so seductive, so attractive, so perfectly tailored to the selfish core of the human heart. It promises everything, but all it delivers is tainted. It's the greatest piece of con-artistry in our world today, and we fall for it in our millions. Men fall for it. Women fall for it. Homes are broken by it. The pain it brings to homes, families, communities, churches and nations is far more destructive than cancer, AIDS or any other illness. Me is the most lethal disease of all.

In its place, Jesus offers commitment to God, the way of the disciple, the path of self-sacrifice. God's love in Jesus is the supreme example and it both offers, and brings, the wonderful realization that I am accepted as I am: a sinner, yes, but a forgiven sinner whose gifts and talents can find no higher fulfilment than being offered back to him in thanksgiving. More than 50 years ago I first discovered that truth for myself and nothing, absolutely nothing has ever matched it for the fulfilment it brought, and still brings. To say 'yes' and 'thank you' to that man on the cross is to take the letter 'I' and to cross it out. Do that, and the Myth of Me begins to lose its attraction. Try it!

19 The Dirtiest Word of All

I feel sorry for Humanists around Christmas. However secular the great binge has become in Christian eyes, for them the religious element is still far too intrusive. Recently, I even saw a newspaper advert offering 'religion-free' holidays for Humanists who want to be shot of it all.

The point was well, if sadly, illustrated for me some years ago in a large supermarket, where I was standing in the checkout queue behind two girls, aged about 20. 'What are you doing for Christmas?' said one. 'What is there to do?' said the other. 'There's nothing to do except get drunk!' It must be a hell of a world when that's all that's left and you're only 20 years old!

What is the alternative? According to St Paul, it is all to do with being saved. There's hardly a more shocking word in contemporary English. Being saved? That's only for nutters, for cults, for fundamentalists, surely?

Absolutely! No normal, average, decent English man or woman would ever use the word. Why, it would bring a blush to the purest English virgin who might never bat an eyelid at uttering your average four-letter word! Shock, horror. The Vicar's said a dirty word. He said 'saved'. How awful!

All right, so I've said it, just like Jesus, Peter, James, Paul and all the Church Fathers, just like the Old Testament, the New Testament, the Book of Common Prayer, the Thirty-Nine Articles, the Queen's Accession Service, the Consecration of Bishops and the Ordination of Priests. What a collection of obscene books and dirty-mouthed Christians and every one of them going on about 'salvation' and 'being saved'.

And to think that sometimes they even use such filthy words in church. Why, even St Paul once had the nerve to write: 'Everyone who calls on the name of the Lord will be saved.'[1] Actually, St Paul was quoting from an ancient Jewish prophet, Joel. Why?

One of the purposes of St Paul's great letter to the Romans (and some of his other letters also) was to make plain to all his readers and hearers that Jesus of Nazareth, crucified and risen from the dead, was God's great and final word to all humanity, Jew and Gentile alike. He knew that the whole world had gone astray; people were out of fellowship with God and needed to be saved from themselves and from the just and certain judgement which a true and holy God must inevitably pronounce on them if his moral integrity was to mean anything. Being saved means establishing a new and creative relationship with the Divine Creator, and men and women who are honest with themselves know that they haven't a hope of achieving that under their own steam. Being saved means recognizing that someone else has got to put things right and that is what, uniquely, Jesus of Nazareth did.

Thirty years ago, Dr Visser't Hooft, the Dutch General Secretary of the World Council of Churches, put it like this. 'The Church,' he announced, 'does not apologize for the fact that it wants all men to know Jesus Christ and to follow him.'[3] Our very calling 'is to proclaim the Gospel to the ends of the earth.' He added that the kind of Christianity which thinks of itself 'as one of many diverse contributions to the religious life of mankind' is a Christianity 'that has lost its foundation in the New Testament'.[4]

This was perfectly normal language for a Christian world leader of the 1960s. Today it sounds wildly restrictive. Why is that? Could it be that more and more people these days have been conned by the secularists and humanists into watering down the claims of the New Testament? I have no doubt that this is so. What, today, the media dismiss as 'fundamentalism' is not just the strict fundamentalism of 70 years ago, with its six-day-creation literalism. No, today all the key Christian doctrines concerning God, Jesus, the incarnation, the cross, the resurrection and the final judgement are lumped together and written off as fundamentalism.

I am not, and never have been, a literal fundamentalist, but in the new dismissive sense I am certainly a fundamentalist. I believe in a God who is both loving and morally holy and acknowledge Jesus of Nazareth as true God and true man. The only good news there is for humanity is God's coming down into our corrupt world in the person of Christ, who will return to judge both the living and the dead. I believe that Christianity is right to claim that a moral God calls for moral absolutes and will not condone humanity's selfishness and greed. Above all, I believe that in his coming, his life, death, resurrection and ascension, Christ gives meaning to existence; he provides an integrated philosophy which makes better sense than the alternatives, and, most importantly, offers hope for eternity. If all that – the common heritage of the Christian Church – is a lot of codswallop, I'll still take the risk of accepting it – and I'll be in very good company. It makes the Myth of Me look like the pathetic sham it is.

One of my most distinguished predecessors as a Canon of St Paul's Cathedral, Henry Liddon, who died more than 100 years ago, was a famous preacher. It was said that he was 'like a trumpet, telling of righteousness and temperance and judgment, preaching ever and always, with personal passion of belief, of Jesus Christ and him crucified'.[5] Such words are not often used of today's preachers. I wonder why?

If the great truths of the gospel are in danger of being lost to our Western nations, either through ignorance or fear of ridicule, how are we to rediscover them? St Paul puts the same question: 'How can they call on one they have not believed in? How can they believe, if they have not heard? How can they hear unless someone preaches?'[6]

This is the task, not just of the clergy, but of every Christian. Jesus Christ alone brings new life, new meaning and new hope. In both the pain and uncertainty of economic recessions, when hopes pinned on material success collapse, and in times of rampant money-making, Jesus stands as firm as a rock. 'Go into all the world and make disciples of all nations.'[7] That is our mandate.

The message is there in the Bible for all to see. That's where we discover the shape, terms and significance of God's good news. Have you attempted to grasp and master it? If you are too busy to do this, your priorities are wrong.

This is what the Bible says to us in the words of St Paul as he continues his theme: 'If you confess with your mouth "Jesus is Lord" and believe in your heart that God raised him from the dead, you will be saved. It is with your heart that you believe and are justified and it is with your mouth that you confess and are saved.'[8]

Paul had no time for secret or vague would-be believers who constantly hedge their bets for fear of being laughed at or, worse still, ignored. He offers his readers a clear choice. Believe inwardly and declare your faith publicly. That's what's missing from our nation and many other Western countries today.

Of course there are questions and uncertainties, but when a man needs to be saved from drowning he doesn't quibble about what the lifebelt or the rope is made of. He grabs and hangs on. If he waits until he's proved everything to his complete satisfaction, he'll drown, and he'll deserve to drown, too, because of his lack of trust in the one who tried to save him.

St Paul's Cathedral is named after the apostle who trusted in Jesus and who, more clearly than any other, showed us how to react to the crucified Christ, whom the grave could not hold. I admire this cathedral; I marvel at its proportions, its architecture, its music and its liturgy. I am proud to serve here, but God is not going to judge me on the quality of my aesthetic sense. It's the good news that 'Jesus saves' that I have to accept or dismiss. That's the ultimate reason why the great Cathedral was built, and if those who work in it forget this, the time will have come to pull it down.

20 Back to Basics

Just suppose that I were to commission a survey to find out what were the four things that most people wanted to avoid in life. I have a strong suspicion that I wouldn't be far wrong if I were to guess in advance that the four things would be more or less as follows:

1 People wouldn't want to have an empty bank account.
2 They wouldn't want an empty freezer.
3 They wouldn't want to have to face sorrow and sadness.
4 They wouldn't want to feel shut out or to be unpopular.

These four are what you might call 'human universals'. Nobody wants to be disliked, to be in pain, to starve or to be broke. Nobody. It applies all over the world. No matter what their race, gender, religion or politics, no one wants to face any of those four things. Of course, many people do have to put up with one or more of them, because it's a rough, tough world out there and life is often unfair.

Then, one day, into this unfair old world comes a man called Jesus. Why did he come? Listen to some people and you would think that his chief task was to give us a lollipop called 'consolation'. (Religion, in the eyes of such people, is no more than the hope of 'pie in the sky when you die, by and by', a soft, sweet con to keep the poor, ill-treated peasants (and especially the wives and mothers) happy and uncomplaining.) However, when the gospel of Jesus began to spread around the towns of Syria, Turkey and Greece, the reaction was not: 'Oh, how lovely and comforting – just what we've always wanted.' No, it wasn't anything of the kind!

Do you remember what happened? Paul and his team were hauled up before the law and the charge was 'turning the world upside down'.[1] So what on earth had they said and done? They had simply taught what Jesus had taught. He was arrested for preaching, and so were they. So what was it that Jesus and his followers said to upset people?

As I have already mentioned, people sometimes tell me that what they like about Jesus is the Sermon on the Mount and the beautiful and comforting Beatitudes. I respond by advising them to read Luke's version of that sermon.[2] If they do, one thing is absolutely certain: they will not find it either 'beautiful' or 'comforting', even if they read it in a traditional version. Should they try it in a modern translation, they just might grasp the fact that seventeenth-century English words can mask and soften the harshness of it.

Try the comparison yourself. 'Blessed are you poor, yours is the Kingdom of God . . .', 'Woe to you that are full now, for you shall hunger' and so on. The Roman Catholic Jerusalem Bible, on the other hand, has: 'How happy are you poor; how happy, you who are hungry, how happy you who weep; how happy, when people hate you and drive you out. Alas for you who are rich, alas for you who laugh' and so on. Take another version, the Good News Bible: 'Happy are you poor, happy are you who are hungry, happy are you who weep; happy are you when people hate you, reject you' – much the same. Then take William Barclay's translation:

Oh the bliss of you who are destitute: Oh the bliss of you who are hungry; of you who weep. Yours

104

is this bliss when men hate you and shut the door
in your face. But tragic is the fate of you who are
rich, you who have eaten your fill, you who laugh,
you when everyone sings your praises.

There isn't much sweetness or consolation here, is
there? These are the 'beautiful' Beatitudes, revealed in
their stark reality. That's what Jesus taught. He upended
the values of our world and they hated him for it.

In the 1960s Dr Joseph McCabe, an American college
President from the Midwest, claimed that 'The major
heresy of the Christian church is not that it obscures the
gospel but that it makes church membership too easy.
We have,' he said, 'developed a Christianity without
discipleship.'[3] The teachings of Jesus, and especially his
Beatitudes, are all about the quality of life which is
meant to mark out the members of the Kingdom.

Let's unpack those disturbing sayings a bit more.
Take the first: 'Oh the bliss of you who are destitute'.[4]
Now, there really is no pleasure in being destitute.
Incidentally, in case you think that this is too melodra-
matic a word, there are two Greek words for poverty.
One means having nothing superfluous, enough just to
scrape by. The other means having absolutely nothing.
This is the word used in Luke's Gospel. When Jesus
refers to the 'bliss' of having absolutely nothing, the
point he is making is that being a member of the Kingdom means total dependency on God. We in the West
are not poor. We are in the top 2 per cent of the world
as regards our standard of living and we tie up all our
wealth in property and possessions. We give the Church
the absolute minimum that we dare and we accept,
often quite uncritically, the values and the material
standards of our secular, selfish, materialistic world. We
do it without thinking, most of the time. By contrast, I
remember an old man who told me 40 years ago that
true happiness was measured in the number of things
you could do without. He was a happy man.

105

Take the second Beatitude. 'Oh the bliss of you who are hungry'.[5] Hunger is a terrible experience. I have been really hungry only once in my life: when I was 20, I went without food for a mere 24 hours. I was in the Army in West Africa and we were out in the bush with, literally, nothing to eat and nowhere to buy any food. However, Jesus uses the word for 'starving', not just 'peckish'. There's no pleasure in starving, yet Jesus used that word. We stuff ourselves full, not just with food and drink, but with art and music and every enjoyable cultural experience. What Jesus wants is followers who will, when necessary, be absolutely free of slavery, even to life's good things. He doesn't just want people who turn their backs on sin, on the evil in life and on marginal things: he wants followers whose scale of values overturns dependency on all material obsessions. Whatever gets in God's way has to take second place. This certainly turns the world's values upside-down.

So the catalogue continues. Jesus's third hammer-blow concerns sorrow. 'Oh the bliss ... of you who weep'.[6] Who wants pain, grief and sorrow in this life? Our values tell us to avoid poverty, starvation and sorrow and, if they come, to blame God! 'Why me, God?' Jesus, on the other hand, is calling for followers who trust him, who are joyful, come what may, because they know that God is ultimately working for the eternal good of his people. The world hates such trust; it wants to shake its fist at God.

As for the last Beatitude, about social rejection:[7] who wants to be rejected, hated, insulted? This is how every true prophet was treated. It's bliss, says Jesus, so cheer up. You will have a rich reward.

Then he goes on to the offensive, stressing the tragic fate that lies in wait for the rich, the over-filled, the laughing boys and girls, the people whom everyone praises. The rich have had all the comforts they will ever get; the people who have eaten their fill will know the pangs of starvation. Those who are always laughing will feel anguish, and the much-praised will recall that their forebears were false prophets.

Thus the fate of the self-centred and self-satisfied is to be (as the Greek text says) 'hissed off the stage'. Jesus did use shock tactics. He often used hyperbole and was very rarely bland or obvious, but he made his point. The values of his followers were to be radically different from those of normal society.

Forgive me for grinding on so. I'd much rather not remind you (or myself) of the unpalatable fact that Jesus of Nazareth was a trouble-maker who offered his followers, not short-term rewards and sweet consolation, but the hatred of the rest of mankind. He knew that they would be regarded as masochistic paragons of self-discipline or dangerously subversive. If it's any consolation, that fellow Jesus got his come-uppance. So did most of his first disciples. No one wanted all the discipleship stuff about hunger and poverty, sorrow and unpopularity. Fortunately, as time went by, the Church managed to smooth off Jesus's rough edges and make his harsh old gospel a bit more enjoyable, so Christians could focus on their great architecture and glorious music. Yes, we got rid of the grit and turned it all into a beautiful pearl.

In recent years the politicians have been talking a lot about 'Getting back to basics.' Yes, of course. When the Church is full of beauty, tolerance and smiles all round, well, that's when the Kingdom will come, won't it?

Pity about that man Jesus though. Unfortunately, he's been asked to stay outside. We can't have him spoiling things, can we?

21 OHMS

Somebody has to do it. Many people would like to do it. The ambitious may well covet it. It's a demanding but highly prestigious and very well-paid occupation. Among the perks are beautiful houses, magnificent cars – maybe even an aeroplane or a helicopter – a large salary, an extensive expense account, servants, free boxes at the opera and so on. In this country knighthoods and the highest honours are among the rewards.

So what am I talking about? I'm talking about the post of ambassador. As defined by *The Shorter Oxford English Dictionary*, an ambassador is 'a minister of the highest rank who represents his sovereign or nation'. From time immemorial, men (and, more recently, women also) have been sent to other nations, given diplomatic safeguards and privileges, and charged with representing, in both directions, the wishes of each to the other. It's one of the meanings given for the letters 'OHMS', On Her Majesty's Service.

No one is fit to be, or likely to be appointed, an ambassador if he doesn't know the mind and the policies of his own nation's rulers. Similarly, no ambassador is likely to be successful, or respected, if he doesn't make every effort to understand the history, culture, and politics of the nation to whom he is sent. Many years ago an American, Joe Kennedy, came to this country as ambassador to the Court of St James. He disliked us, distrusted us and misrepresented us to his President and Congress. He did not last long in this post, but he caused much damage and could have created a world-wide catastrophe had he not been recalled in time and replaced by someone who rebuilt mutual confidence and saved the situation from disaster. The successful ambassador does not sell his own country short, but he does his utmost to build bridges of trust wherever possible.

In our modern world there are perhaps three kinds of ambassador. The first is, inevitably, political. He builds contacts between nations through governments. He may need to convey unpopular information and if so he will not shrink from it. He is sometimes faced with personal moral dilemmas. Truth and loyalty may come into collision. Four hundred years ago the task of an ambassador was defined as being that of 'an honest man sent abroad to lie for the good of his country'.[2] The post of ambassador may be a well-paid and prestigious one, but for an honest man it will always bring pressure on his conscience.

The second kind of ambassador may be either an individual or a group. He, she or they may be sportsmen, musicians, artists – indeed almost anyone who, by their actions and attitudes, interprets and commends their homeland, skills and life-style to others.

In 1992, the winners of gold and silver medals in the Olympic 10,000 metres race for women fought out a battle on the track for half the race. One was a white South African, the other a black Ethiopian. Their attitude to each other in victory and defeat was a powerful lesson. They were ambassadors for athletics, ambassadors for tough competition, but above all ambassadors for magnanimity in victory and defeat.

There is also a third kind of ambassador and this is the one commended by St Paul. Three times in his letters he describes himself by that title, calling himself an 'ambassador for Christ'[3] and an 'ambassador for the gospel'.[4] His task, he tells us, has three aspects and they are the same for every Christian who accepts Christ's call to be a faithful servant. If I call myself a follower of Jesus, this is my charter, just as it was Paul's.

The first aspect concerns the character of the person. When Paul uses the word to the Corinthians he says that the Christian ambassador must live the kind of life that puts no stumbling-blocks in the way of other people.[5] In other words, a 'quality' life, free from moral and personal blemish. This, you might say, rules out all of us, but that's a cop-out. None of us is perfect, but what counts is motive: do you want to be a good, holy, righteous person? That's what God wants: not second-raters, content to do the minimum, but 'out-and-outers' who accept God's challenge. Paul adds that such Christian ambassadors will be roughly handled by the world and that only by patient endurance, like that of Jesus, will they be effective ambassadors.

The second aspect concerns not just the character of the person, but the content of the message. An ambassador has things to say. He is there to be God's voice. Yes, that's what Paul actually says: 'as though God himself were speaking through us'.[6] When we speak about Christ, or when we preach for Christ, as long as we faithfully pass on the message as the New Testament sets it out, we are God's voice. So a sermon, if it truly represents Christ's teaching, is God speaking, not just the vicar 'sounding off'. Of course if any preacher uses the pulpit merely to push his own opinions or prejudices, that's quite another matter. However, if we take care to ground our preaching in the words of the New Testament gospel, we are genuinely becoming, as Paul says, God's voice to the hearer. As you read this book, you must ask whether what I say is the true message of Scripture or not. If it is, then, like the dog in the old HMV adverts, you are hearing your Master's voice and God will expect you to obey it. That is a tremendous pressure on a preacher. He must do all he can to ensure that what he says is truly God's word, not merely a sermon knocked up in a hurry to fill time in a service.

And what exactly is the content, according to Paul? It is a message about a merciful God, who sent his son to die for us, to free us from the sin which disfigures our lives. 'You,' says Paul, 'need to stop being God's enemies and, by accepting his forgiveness become his friends.'[7] When you have accepted that free gift of forgiveness, don't waste your life. Use it to pass on that same Good News to others.

Finally, there is the challenge of the task. The Christian ambassador is to plead and fearlessly make known, as persuasively as he can, Christ's Good News. He is to be bold, not hesitant. Christ's love compels him. So says St Paul.

Not long ago I discovered a very sad fact. One of the greatest and most powerful of Charles Wesley's hymns, a hymn which I hope they will sing at my funeral one day, ends with these poignant and potent words, the true preacher's charter:

> His only righteousness I show, his saving grace
> proclaim,
> 'Tis all my business here below to cry 'Behold,
> the Lamb'.
> Happy, if with my latest breath, I might but
> gasp his Name,
> Preach him to all, and cry in death, behold,
> behold the Lamb.[8]

That wonderful hymn is missing in four out of six of the hymn-books most recently published in the UK and in all the latest American ones I have seen as well.

Can it be that our churches today are ashamed to be ambassadors for Christ, ashamed to accept the Master's charge to live for him, speak for him, suffer for him and proclaim him Saviour and Lord? That task is not an optional extra for you or me. It is built right into the very Good News. If there is Good News for a fallen world, there must be people to tell the Good News, ambassadors, men and women filled with that same Spirit as those who took the message of a crucified, risen and living Jesus out into the old Roman world and conquered it with God's love.

Today, God still needs ambassadors.

PART 5

Heading for the Chequered Flag

22 A Hell of a Way to Go

Jesus called Hell 'outer darkness'[1] and spoke of it as a place where human beings would grind their teeth in utter hopelessness and weep in desolation. Not a pretty picture, is it?

Some time ago I was lunching with the managing director of one of our largest commercial empires. He wasn't, I think, a Christian, but he stopped me in my tracks by asking me quite bluntly, 'Why has the Church given up its belief in Hell?' I told him that I didn't think that it had and added that I certainly hadn't, and he seemed surprised and pleased. Still, he had a point. There's no doubt that the English have, by and large, given up on Hell and they think themselves very civilized to have done so. Newspaper polls maintain that less than a quarter of the adult population believe in such an idea. Illogically, about three-quarters still believe in Heaven (which is, when you stop and consider, mere wishful thinking). It makes sense to believe in both or in neither. However, when you look at all the evil in the world you may wonder where they're going to find enough perfect people to occupy Heaven.

I was reminded of this by the irritating spectacle of a Government minister accusing the Church of failing to provide guidance about 'right and wrong'. As the great majority of people in the UK today don't go to church regularly, how would they know what we clergy teach? They read it in the newspapers. So how do journalists know? Most of them don't go to church. If 99 out of every 100 vicars preach thoroughly orthodox sermons on Christian faith and morals week after week, no journalist will bother to tell you. It only needs one unorthodox vicar to say something outrageous and every journalist will print his ravings. As they say, 'Man bites dog is news; Dog bites man isn't'. So British people (and that includes Government ministers) are only ever told what the idiots, the extremists and the naughty boys say or get up to. As a result, the non-church-going nation, and its politicians, assume that the Church spends all its time teaching heresy, political revolution or a moral free-for-all. That is arrant nonsense, but, although the latest surveys tell us that the clergy are among the most trusted people in the community (and the politicians and journalists among the least trusted), people still believe what they read in the newspapers. Yes, even Government ministers, who ought to know better.

Take my own experience. I have been preaching biblical orthodoxy and biblical ethics for over forty years. Have the media noticed? Never. But I have had three or four major brushes with the media in the past twenty years. Not once have I said anything wild or irresponsible. I still stand by it all. But I once edited a hymnbook which modernized some old-fashioned language.[2] I once wrote a highly moral book about Christian teenage sexual ideals.[3] I once erected an a-symmetrical contemporary churchyard notice board. In all three cases the newspapers produced total caricatures of what I had said and done. Suddenly, Members of Parliament and the public leapt upon me and savaged me solely because of what the papers had written. They ignored all those years of faithful biblical preaching and instantly believed a pack of lies trotted out by a pack of liars. It's hardly surprising then if the Church gets blamed when things go wrong in the nation. We have

116

fought to keep England Christian for generations and we've been ignored or sneered at. Now, when what we warned would happen is coming true, lo and behold, it's all our fault! What nauseating hypocrisy!

The English want some lessons on right and wrong, do they? Well, here's one – don't blame me if you don't like it. Each year in December comes the season called 'Advent', when the theme of the Last Judgement and of Heaven and Hell is uppermost in the Church's lectionary and hymns. My lunch companion thought we had stopped believing in Hell. Of course, some Anglicans here and in other parts of the world have, but most (like myself) haven't. Richard Niebuhr spoke trenchantly of those whose gospel had been so reduced that: 'a God without wrath brought men without sin into a kingdom without judgment through the ministrations of a Christ without a cross'.[4]

John Steinbeck, the novelist, attacks churches whose 'psychiatric priesthood' explains that sin isn't really sin but accidents set in motion by forces beyond our control. Steinbeck tells of a preacher he heard in Vermont 'with tool-steel eyes' who spoke of 'a well-stoked, white-hot hell served by technicians of the first order. Nowhere', says Steinbeck, 'did I find the quality of that preacher. He forged a religion designed to last.'[5]

We are instinctively repelled by the very idea of answerability, of judgement, of Hell. We shut our eyes to evil, individual and corporate, except in the most extreme cases, and back off from the thought that a holy God (and what good is any other kind?) might take a tough line with people who, having wrecked his earth, would doubtless wreck his heaven, given half a chance. We blandly excuse everything, each breaking of the Ten Commandments, every broken marriage, our betrayal of children, honour and trust, and we tell God that our lack of moral fibre is not our fault, but that of

117

the Church (which we have ignored). We insist that God owes us an eternity, not of judgement, but of delectable bliss.

I shall never forget a remark my first vicar made at the local cemetery. A funeral director arrived with the coffin of the deceased, who had never been near a church. 'I hear,' said the director, 'that he was a good man.' The vicar looked sceptically at him. 'Where,' he asked 'do they bury the bad ones?'

What does the Bible say about Hell? That's where we need to go to find solid roots for our Christian theology. The first thing we note is that the concept of Hell is not based on just one word or idea. In both Old and New Testaments the words 'Sheol' (in Hebrew) and 'Hades' (in Greek) mean no more than 'the place of the dead', shadowy, empty, colourless and hopeless, a monotonous existence of grey gloom. After Christ's resurrection, Paul taunted death because Christ had drawn its sting and death had lost its old power. Christ has been there and proclaimed the victory of the Cross. When our Creed says 'he descended into Hell' it means that Jesus declared his triumph to the dead.

Another, totally separate and much more terrifying, idea is one that is unique to Jesus himself. Outside Jerusalem there was a huge permanent bonfire, a burning rubbish-tip. It was called the Valley of Hinnom, or 'Gehenna'.[8] Jesus used it as a symbol of ultimate destruction for those who put themselves first, whether they were religious or not. That image stuck in people's minds and it was later portrayed and caricatured with devils and toasting forks. But Jesus used other imagery to describe Hell: he spoke of flood, darkness, a wine-press and so on. Whatever the imagery, the root idea remained and still forms the core of the Christian doctrine of judgement: the experience of rejection. God, the loving one, seeks humanity, dies for humanity, but

118

never overrides our freedom to reject him. He gives us the right to choose for ourselves, whatever the consequences. The theme is vividly portrayed in Marlowe's *Dr Faustus* and in Mozart's *Don Giovanni*. Faustus and Giovanni both end in hell, having chosen to disobey God quite deliberately.

C. S. Lewis once put it memorably: 'God in his mercy made the fixed pains of Hell that misery might be stayed.'[9] In short, what we sow, we reap. There is a fixed and clear-cut price and if that's what you want, that's what you get. All life offers moral choice and moral accountability is part of the deal. If you want free will, you answer for your choices. In the words of an old Spanish proverb, '"Take what you want," says God, "take it – and pay."'

Consider the contrast between C. S. Lewis and D. H. Lawrence. In three of his poems, Lawrence speaks in horror of the bottomless abyss of emptiness in which human beings, 'god-lost creatures', like a 'fizzling falling rocket' endlessly writhe in the ultimate, terrible self-knowledge which eternity brings and which never ends.[10] C. S. Lewis's picture is indeed truly merciful when set against this.

Hell, eternal self-isolation, is what Rodin's famous figure of 'The Thinker' contemplates in his great sculpture 'The Gates of Hell'. Most people assume that The Thinker is merely a dispassionate philosopher. Not so. Seated on top of the gates of Hell, he watches as human beings – all alone and self-obsessed – fall into the abyss. We human beings will do anything, as Joseph Conrad said, 'to escape from the grim shadow of self-knowledge'.[11] We can't bear to face up to God's total awareness of our self-centred souls. Yet St John, in his Gospel, speaks of Jesus dying so that we should not perish (we who deserve it), but have eternal life.[12] Christ's death paid the price of sin required by a holy God and opened up that glorious eternity which we call 'Heaven' for those who trust that he, and he alone, is the Saviour that all humanity needs.

Hell and damnation are not the heart of the Christian message, thank God! They are the backdrop against which the drama of human salvation is played out. As a modern man, a twentieth-century man, I might wish that they weren't present in the Bible, especially in the teaching of Jesus. It would be so much easier, and more popular, if the preacher offered only sweetmeats, the soft, sticky, Turkish delight which people love to hear, about hope, forgiveness, love and Heaven.

But Hell and damnation are there. I can only jettison this tough element of Christian theology if I do violence to what Jesus taught and the meaning of what he – the Son of God – did.

I can't do that. How about you?

23 *Dust to Dust*

It is not exactly a secret that I'm dying. I haven't any obvious illness or symptoms, and I feel fine. Nevertheless, it's a plain fact: I'm dying. So, of course, are you. For some strange reason, most people dare not admit it. To talk openly about death is to send shock waves through everyone present.

Three or four years ago I was preaching at a large festival service in Bolton in Lancashire. At the end, I stood by the door saying goodbye to the congregation. A very old lady came past and said to me, 'As I was sat there, I said to myself, "How sad that that young man must die".' Since I was over 60 at the time, I was flattered by the 'young man' bit. She was absolutely right. I was indeed going to die and since, as a famous Dean of St Paul's Cathedral, John Donne, once said: 'Any man's death diminishes me,' she was also right to say that it was sad. 'Never,' said Donne, 'send to know for whom the bell tolls; it tolls for thee.'[1]

Death is the great universal. No one escapes it. Even Jesus Christ died. It comes in many different ways. In this country, so I'm told, one in five of us dies suddenly. Three-quarters of a million of us die in any given year. Some die young, some die old. Some die quietly, peacefully, others in terrible or horrible circumstances. The manner and the time varies, but the fact is the one certainty. 'Death,' as St Paul once said, 'is the last enemy.'[2]

The clergy preach about death quite often, of course,

121

but not, I suspect, at ordinary Sunday services. We conduct hundreds of funerals, at which everyone is expecting to hear something on the subject in the very presence of the coffin of a friend or loved one. In the context of a Sunday morning service, I don't suppose I've preached more than a dozen sermons in 40 years of ministry. Many of my brother and sister clergy may well have avoided the theme completely. This is one of the problems we face today. Death has, for many people, become the great unmentionable, the one real obscenity in modern life. It is, perhaps, one of the inevitable consequences of our society's loss of Christian faith that, on film and television and in our newspapers, we see death paraded all over our world day by day, but it shocks us only when it bursts upon us in acts of meaningless madness, or when children kill other children or young men kill feeble 90-year-olds with horrifying brutality.

In a century that has seen mass murder on an industrial scale, we can get angry about violent homicide and yet when death, ordinary death (if I can so describe it) happens, we are numbed and silenced. Often we look for someone to blame. 'I can't believe in God,' a middle-aged woman said to me some years ago. 'He let my dad die.' Her father was in his eighties and had died, peacefully, of heart failure, the most common cause of death in our society. 'God let me down,' she said angrily. It was natural, and right, for her to be sad, but her real problem was not God. It was her unwillingness to face the universal fact that we all die. She was living in a fantasy-land.

Some time ago I was talking to a doctor and said, just in passing, 'I'm in my middle sixties now. I'll soon be in injury time.' 'You mustn't think like that,' the doctor told me. 'Why?' I replied. 'That way I'm being absolutely realistic. After three score years and ten, whatever I get is a bonus. I'll be grateful. Life expectancy for men in this country is 74. Why get upset?'

122

But, you might say, ought we to be philosophical about it? Should we not, like Dylan Thomas, 'rage, rage against the dying of the light'? Is it a weakness merely to accept that we shall die? Should we not, like Dylan Thomas, urge the dying (ourselves included) not to 'go gentle into that good night'?[3] I can understand this attitude, and sympathize with it, if I perceive death as the end of everything. 'To die,' as Shakespeare's Claudio says, 'and go we know not where, to lie in cold obstruction and to rot'.[8]

That fear, of a slow disintegration and an unknown destination, is a strong one, and it is logical enough. People invent a nice after-life and assume they will go on in suburban leafy bliss, though it isn't clear why, or what there will be to do, and they always assume they will be in the best of health with all their wants fully met. It's fantasy-land. It also assumes that death wipes out all our responsibility, leaving us answerable for nothing. Such illusions are morally debilitating and self-obsessed. It assumes that somehow I am worth keeping even for eternity when my body's sell-by date is long past.

What a contrast that is with the Christian attitude to death! Jesus faced death knowing that he would come again to give us an eternal destiny, that he would break the power of death and take away humanity's fear of the grave.

'Mere words,' retorts the sceptic. 'Anyone can say that – it's just as much a fantasy as all the rubbish people talk about an after-life.' Now, I am inclined to agree with the sceptic that it's all wishful thinking. Unless . . . . Just suppose that man Jesus did, in reality, rise from the dead. Then his words take on a wholly new and vital meaning. Archbishop Michael Ramsey put it so simply, in just four words: 'No resurrection: no Christianity.'[5]

In his first letter to the Church in Corinth, St Paul puts this point as bluntly as anyone ever has: 'If Christ didn't rise from the dead we, and all who have believed in him, are utterly lost, our gospel is null and void.'[6] That's the negative side. But then he turns the tables and declares, without hesitation, 'but the truth is that Christ was raised to life – the first fruits of the harvest of the dead.'[7] That's a tremendous metaphor isn't it? A harvest of the dead, rising like waving corn, to new life. Those who belong to Christ, who are members of his fellowship and who have placed their trust in him, will make up this great harvest. In what have they trusted? Paul spells it out: they believe and trust that Christ died for their sins, that he was raised to life for them and that, by his grace, they too will share in that resurrection. That, says St Paul, is the Good News which transforms every Christian. That is the Good News which Christians proclaim.

Writing to the Romans, he adds that not even death 'can separate us from the love of God in Christ Jesus'[8] and in his Letter to the Philippians again he stresses that he would rather die and be with Christ than live. Living, he reminds Christians, we are with Christ but 'to depart and be with Christ – that is better by far.'[9]

Everything hinges, therefore, on whether or not Christ rose from the dead. If he did (and I've gambled my life on it), the knowledge that I'm dying – however long it takes to happen – is a cause for hope, for joy, for relaxation. I'm in God's hands and I trust them.

So, when I say I'm dying, I mean it. Death is welcome, because it's the gateway to eternity with my loving Father. That confident hope in eternity is one of our great privileges as Christians. I hope you have that confidence. Christ freely offers it to you.

24 Are You . . . ?

We're not quite finished. We have to go back to that business of 'being saved'. Paul tells his friends that God has 'destined us . . . for the full attainment of salvation',[1] and warns them to be alert and ready for Christ's return, awake and sober, in order that they may 'enter fully into the possession of salvation'.

Sneering at, or being embarrassed by, such language is, of course, one of the Devil's best weapons. C. S. Lewis's demonic character, Screwtape, tells his junior colleague, Wormwood, to work on his charge so that he 'will quite easily believe that the Christian religion is somehow ridiculous'[2] because of the eccentricities of some who profess it. Wormwood is to foster an attitude of flippancy, which is 'the finest armour-plating'[3] against God. Getting people to sneer at the idea of salvation is the best possible way to keep them from giving serious thought to the meaning of life.

So, if you can persuade people that there is no ultimate meaning to life, you can trap them into one of four attitudes which will remove, in their eyes, any sense of divine purpose:

1 Persuade them that life is merely a cycle of rebirths, leading nowhere.
2 Persuade them that humanity is getting better and better and will ultimately reach some kind of moral perfection.
3 Depress them into thinking that, because we

shall all disintegrate in a cosmic Big Bang, there is no goal or meaning to life.

4 Best of all, encourage them to believe that God is a divine wimp without moral virtue who will overlook all that is evil or selfish, patting humanity on the head, and doling out eternal Christmas presents. People love that idea best of all because it can be camouflaged under the treacle-trap of words like 'the love of God'.

None of these four approaches requires anything so demeaning as salvation. 'Salvation' implies rescue: a lifeboat for the drowning, a saviour for the helpless. No, thank you, we don't want that. It would put us in debt to God and make us dependent on him. We much prefer to be self-made men and proud of it.

Unfortunately, the Christian gospel is Good News of just such a Saviour. His very name, Jesus (or Yeshua in Hebrew), means 'saviour', or 'deliverer'. He came, and will return, to deliver and save us. The three words 'save', 'saviour' and 'salvation' are mentioned 259 times in the Old Testament and 115 times in the New Testament, not counting all the other words with the same, or a similar, meaning. The theme of salvation is absolutely integral to the Bible's message, from start to finish, from Genesis to Revelation.

Beautiful architecture, art, music or any form of beauty known to man – these alone cannot save you, or me or any human being. These external adornments are mere decoration of a corpse if there is no salvation. To say that, is, of course, deeply offensive to our human desire for self-righteousness, self-justification, self-satisfaction and self-confidence. We long for our achievements and attainments to justify us in the sight of God. We want to say 'I've done my best', and think that that will be good enough in God's eyes. At that point to be told that I am a sinner, in need of a Saviour, frighteningly undermines one's pride. Yet that is the heart and core of the Christian gospel.

But what about the idea of St Paul's that we can enter fully into the possession of salvation? Isn't this an appallingly self-righteous idea? It could well seem to be unless it is properly understood, as Paul realized. He was careful to use a whole range of tenses in order to make the point absolutely clear.

There is a well-known story about a brash young undergraduate who burst in on a professor of theology demanding: 'Are you saved?' The professor, so the story goes, said: 'Do you mean *sesosmai, sozomai* or *sothaisomai*?' The professor was gently reminding the objectionable, but well-meaning, student that – in Greek – St Paul uses the word 'saved' in past, present and future tenses. Paul was right. It was absolutely vital to be able to say, as he did to the Ephesians: 'We have been saved'.[4] By this he meant that Christ had achieved our salvation on the cross and, in putting our trust in this act, we can quite rightly say that we have been saved. The transaction has been completed, signed and sealed, as symbolized by baptism. The deed is done.

So, too, in writing to the Corinthians, Paul could say, 'We are being saved'.[5] The deed is done, yet the experience of entering fully into salvation is a lifelong process to be worked through. It is rather like marriage. Getting married is a decisive act, but learning how to make it work is a lifelong process.

Finally, Paul quite properly reminds the Romans that 'we shall be saved'[6] when all is complete. Christ returns to fulfil God's eternal purpose for his creation.

Each of the three tenses used is essential. We are assured that the deed of salvation is done, that there is a real challenge to continue working out the process, and that the good work that has begun will be completed when Christ returns. This threefold meaning is exactly what Paul explains when he writes to the churches.

Salvation, therefore, is a fact, an experience and a coming fulfilment. It offers me the assurance that Christ has made me his; that, through his Spirit, he is daily transforming me to grow more like him, and that Christ will come again to complete the process. Similarly, when the photographer presses the button, the image is fixed. Then the film needs to undergo a developing process. Finally, the print is there, complete and framed, for all to see.

'God,' wrote Paul, 'has not destined us for retribution but for the full attainment of salvation through our Lord Jesus Christ.'[7] It is a tremendous and exciting hope that is offered to us. Christ died for me and I trust in him: he will keep his promise. My feet are on solid ground. Salvation is not a reward for my efforts to be moral. It's a gift to a sinner who needs a Saviour. And I'm not alone. He calls me to be part of his priestly Kingdom, called to serve him and worship him for all eternity.

And that has to be the best good news that the world has ever heard.

These Are the Facts

a hymn written on 6 June 1971

These are the facts as we have received them,
these are the truths that the Christian believes,
this is the basis of all of our preaching,
Christ died for sinners and rose from the tomb.

These are the facts as we have received them,
Christ has fulfilled what the Scriptures foretold.
Adam's whole family in death had been sleeping,
Christ through his rising restores us to life.

These are the facts as we have received them,
we shall be changed in the blink of an eye.
Trumpets shall sound as we face life immortal,
this is the victory through Jesus our Lord.

These are the facts as we have received them,
these are the truths that the Christian believes,
this is the basis of all of our preaching,
Christ died for sinners and rose from the tomb.

MICHAEL SAWARD

References

Bible references are taken (unless otherwise indicated) from the Revised English Bible (1989). Other versions used are indicated as follows:

KJV   King James Version (Authorised Version 1611)
RV   Revised Version (1885)
RSV   Revised Standard Version (1952)
LYC   Letters to Young Churches (Phillips 1947)
JB   Jerusalem Bible (1966)
WB   William Barclay New Testament (1968)
GNB   Good News Bible (1976)

The author's own paraphrases are indicated by MS.

Chapter 1
1 Exact source unknown (Gautama Buddha).
2 Blamires, H., *The Christian Mind*, p. 3, SPCK, 1963.
3 Wells, A. M., *Inspiring Quotations*, no. 2321, Thomas Nelson, 1988.
4 From a paper given to London clergy, 16 September 1993.
5 1 Corinthians 2.16.
6 Romans 12.2, LYC.
7 Orr, J., *The Christian View of God and the World*, p. 20, Andrew Elliot, 1893.
8 Coomes, D., *Dorothy L. Sayers*, p. 214, Lion, 1992.
9 Coomes, D., *Dorothy L. Sayers*, p. 129, Lion, 1992.
10 From a paper to the Anglican Evangelical Assembly, 1995.
11 Chiefly taken from Philippians 2.

Chapter 2
1 Marx, Karl, *Critique of Hegel's Philosophy of Right*, publisher not known, 1843–44.
2 Shaw, G. B., *Plays Pleasant and Unpleasant*, Vol ii, Preface, p. vii, in *Oxford Dictionary of Quotations*, p. 498, no. 11, Book Club Associates, 1981.
3 Matheson, G., hymn, *Gather us in*.
4 *The Listener*, 2 April 1970.
5 Quoted in *The Times*, 5 April 1969.
6 Acts 26.5; Galatians 1.14; James 1.26–27.

130

7   John 1.29, GNB.
8   The Nicene Creed.
9   Amos 5.19–24, MS.
10   Acts 17.23, MS.
11   John 14.6.
12   2 Corinthians 5.17, RSV.
13   Film, *Martin Luther*, 1953.

Chapter 3

1   Psalm 67.
2   Packer, J. I., *Knowing God*, p. 230, Hodder & Stoughton, 1973.
3   Psalm 67.2, GNB (abbreviated).

Chapter 4

1   From The Alternative Service Book 1980, Rite A.
2   From The Alternative Service Book 1980, Rite A.
3   2 Timothy 3.16, MS.
4   2 Timothy 3.16, MS.
5   Barclay, W., *Letters to Timothy, Titus and Philemon*, p. 201, Saint Andrew Press, 1975.
6   House of Bishops, *The Nature of Christian Belief*, p. 6, Church House Publishing, 1986.
7   House of Bishops, *The Nature of Christian Belief*, p. 5, Church House Publishing, 1986.
8   House of Bishops, *The Nature of Christian Belief*, p. 5, Church House Publishing, 1986.
9   House of Bishops, *The Nature of Christian Belief*, p. 6, Church House Publishing, 1986.
10   *Church of England Newspaper*.
11   Wells, A. M., *Inspiring Quotations*, no. 139, Thomas Nelson, 1988.
12   Wells, A. M., *Inspiring Quotations*, no. 148, Thomas Nelson, 1988.
13   Wells, A. M., *Inspiring Quotations*, no. 161, Thomas Nelson, 1988.
14   Green, J. R., *Short History of the English People*, publisher not known, 1874.

Chapter 5

1   Genesis 1.1–2.3.
2   Green, P., *Kenneth Grahame*, John Murray, 1959.
3   Genesis 1.1–2.3.
4   Genesis 2.4–25.
5   Genesis 2.24, RSV.
6   Genesis 1.28, RSV.
7   Book of Common Prayer: Marriage Service.

Chapter 6

1   Interview in *The Guardian*, 24 December 1969.
2   1 Samuel 17.4–54.
3   2 Samuel 11.2–27.

4   Genesis 17.7.
5   Exodus 24.8, 34.10.
6   Hebrews 8.13.

Chapter 7

1   Kung, H., *That the World may Believe*, pp. 103–4, Sheed and Ward, 1963.
2   Blake, William, drawing 'The Ancient of Days'.
3   Michelangelo, painting 'The Creation of Adam'.
4   Calvin, J., *Institutes of the Christian Religion*, 1.11.1., publisher not known, 1536.
5   John 1.18.
6   Ezekiel 1.26–28.
7   Revelation 1.13–18.
8   Revelation 1.17.
9   Revelation 1.17–18.
10 John 1.18.
11 Browning, E. B., *Aurora Leigh*, book ix, publisher not known, 1857.
12 Revelation 4.8.
13 Revelation 4.11.
14 Revelation 5.12, GNB.
15 John 14.6.

Chapter 8

1   Kendrick, G., hymn, *We believe in God the Father*.
2   Acts 8.9.
3   Acts 8.10–11.
4   Acts 8.19.
5   Acts 8.20, MS.
6   Creighton, L., *Life and Letters of Mandell Creighton*, i, 3 April 1887, p. 372, publisher not known, 1904.
7   Machiavelli, N., *Il principe* (The Prince), publisher not known, 1532.
8   *Against Heresies*, Irenaeus, Book V, 2.3.
9   *A Plea*, Athenagoras the Athenian 10 and 24.
10 Genesis 1.2, RV mg.
11 Acts 2.1–4.
12 The Nicene Creed.

Chapter 9

1   *The Virgin Mary had a Baby Boy*, West Indian traditional carol.
2   Machen, J. G., *The Virgin Birth of Christ*, pp. 317–79, James Clarke, 1930.
3   Matthew 1.18–25.
4   Luke 1.26–38.
5   Isaiah 7.14.
6   Matthew 1.23.
7   John 8.4.
8   Interrogatory Creed of Hippolytus c. 215.

9 Letter to the Ephesians 7.20. Ignatius of Antioch c. 107.
10 Letter to the Ephesians 18.2.
11 Letter to the Smyrneans 1.1. Ignatius of Antioch.
12 Ware, K., *The Orthodox Way*, pp. 100–101, Mowbrays, 1979.
13 Apostles' Creed.

Chapter 10
1 1 Kings 6.20.
2 Revelation 21.16.
3 Isaiah 6.5; Jeremiah 1.6–7; Ezekiel 1.28.
4 Isaiah 6.5–7.
5 Mant, R., hymn, *Bright the Vision*.
6 2 Corinthians 5.21, KJV.
7 Hughes, P. E., 2 Corinthians, *New London Commentary*, p. 211, Marshall, Morgan and Scott, 1962.
8 1 Peter 2.24, RSV.
9 1 Peter 3.18, RSV.
10 Leviticus 3.8, RSV.
11 This paragraph is a paraphrase of St Paul's 'gospel'.

Chapter 11
1 Acts 26.1.
2 Acts 12.1–2.
3 Mark 6.16.
4 Matthew 2.1.
5 Josephus, Flavius, *Antiquities of the Jews*, Book XV, Ch. 7, Thomas Nelson, 1883.
6 Matthew 2.1–16.
7 Mark 1.4–8.
8 Matthew 11.2–6, MS.
9 Mark 1.14, MS.
10 Isaiah 9.6–7, GNB.
11 Matthew 13.13–14, MS.
12 Matthew 5–7.
13 Matthew 5.3–10.

Chapter 12
1 See Chapter 11, note 11.
2 Luke 15 throughout this chapter.
3 Shakespeare, W., *Hamlet*, Act I. Scene 3.34 and 105; *Richard II*, Act III. Scene 4.29; *Merchant of Venice*, Act III. Scene 1.41.
4 Luke 15.2–7, MS.
5 *A Dictionary of Modern Quotations*, p. 22, Penguin Books, 1971.
6 Fraser, A., *King Charles II*, p. 371, Book Club Associates, 1979.
7 Donaldson, F., *Edward III: The Road to Abdication*, p. 168, Book Club Associates, 1978.
8 Luke 15.18–19.

Chapter 13

1 See Chapter 2, note 1.
2 Kingsley, C., *Letters to the Chartists*, No. 2, publisher not known.
3 See Chapter 11, note 12.
4 See Chapter 11, note 13.
5 Luke 16.19–31 throughout this chapter.

Chapter 14

1 Tanitch, R., *Dirk Bogarde: The Complete Career*, p. 122, Ebury Press, 1988.
2 *Upstairs, Downstairs*, London Weekend Television serial.
3 Genesis 12.3, MS.
4 Isaiah 53.5, RSV.
5 Isaiah 53.12, GNB.
6 Isaiah 49.3, GNB.
7 Goldingay, J., *God's Prophet: God's Servant*, p. 154, Paternoster Press, 1984.
8 Goldingay, J., *God's Prophet: God's Servant*, p. 154–5, Paternoster Press, 1984.
9 Luke 23.34.
10 Goldingay, J., *God's Prophet: God's Servant*, p. 156, Paternoster Press, 1984.
11 This is the central message of 1 Peter.
12 Luke 22.27, GNB.
13 John 13.16.

Chapter 15

1 Hebrews 9.15 and 12.24.
2 Hebrews 8.6.
3 1 Timothy 2.5, MS.
4 Galatians 3.19–20.
5 Hebrews 9.19–21, quoting Exodus 24.8.
6 Hebrews 9.22.
7 1 Timothy 2.5–6, RSV.
8 See Chapter 10, note 10.
9 Galatians 2.20.
10 See Chapter 2, note 7.

Chapter 16

1 Luke 24 throughout this chapter.
2 Luke 24.46–47, GNB.
3 Forster, E. M., *Howards End*, Penguin, 1992.

Chapter 17

1 Ephesians 1.20, GNB.
2 Apostles' Creed.
3 Revelation 1.5–6.
4 Hebrews 7.25, RSV.

5   Matthew 27.51.
6   Hebrews 9.24, MS.
7   Hebrews 10.12, MS.
8   Hebrews 8.3 and 9.7 especially. See Dimock, N., *Our One High Priest on High*, Longman Green, 1910.
9   Wesley, C., hymn, *Rejoice the Lord is King*.
10   Chrysostom, John, – Homily XIII, *Epistle to the Hebrews*.

Chapter 18
1   Lawson, A., *Adultery*, p. 25, Blackwell, 1989.
2   Lawson, A., *Adultery*, p. 25, Blackwell, 1989.
3   Sartre, J-P., *Huis Clos*, Routledge, 1990.
4   Mark 9.35, MS.
5   Mark 9.42, MS.
6   Mark 8.34, MS.
7   Mark 9.43–48, MS.
8   Mark 12.31.
9   Mark 12.30–31, MS.
10   Matthew 13.45–46.

Chapter 19
1   Romans 10.13.
2   Joel 2.32.
3   Quoted in CMS Newsletter, April 1964.
4   Quoted in CMS Newsletter, April 1964.
5   Carpenter, S. C., *Church and People 1789–1889*, p. 293, SPCK, 1959.
6   Romans 10.14, MS.
7   Matthew 28.19, MS.
8   Romans 10.9, MS.

Chapter 20
1   Acts 17.6, RSV.
2   Luke 6.17–49.
3   Quoted in *Expository Times*, June 1964.
4   Luke 6.20, WB.
5   Luke 6.21, WB.
6   Luke 6.21, WB.
7   Luke 6.22, WB.

Chapter 21
1   *The Shorter Oxford English Dictionary*, Oxford University Press, 1973 edition.
2   Wotton, Sir Henry, *Oxford Dictionary of Quotations*, p. 583, Book Club Associates, 1981.
3   2 Corinthians 5.20 and Philemon 9.
4   Ephesians 6.20.
5   2 Corinthians 6.3.

6   2 Corinthians 5.20, MS.
7   2 Corinthians 5.20, MS.
8   Wesley, C., hymn, *Jesus the Name High Over All.*

Chapter 22
1   Matthew 22.13, RSV.
2   Saward, M., *Hymns for Today's Church*, Hodder & Stoughton, 1982.
3   Saward, M., *And So To Bed?*, Good Reading, 1975.
4   Niebuhr, R., *The Kingdom of God in America*, p. 193, Harper & Row, 1988.
5   Steinbeck, J., *Travels with Charley*, Mandarin, 1995.
6   1 Corinthians 15.55.
7   Apostles' Creed: Book of Common Prayer version.
8   'Gehenna' is used 12 times in the New Testament, all but once in the gospels. The first is Matthew 5.22.
9   Lewis, C. S., *Poems*, p. 98, 'Divine Justice', Geoffrey Bles, 1964.
10 Lawrence, D. H., 'The Hands of God', 'Abysmal Immorality' and 'Only Man', from *Selected Poems*, pp. 122–5, Penguin Books, 1950.
11 Conrad, J., *Lord Jim*. In MacKinnon (ed) *Objections to Christian Belief*, p. 33, Penguin, 1965.
12 John 3.16, MS.

Chapter 23
1   Donne, J., *Meditation XVII.*
2   1 Corinthians 15.26.
3   Thomas, D., *Selected Works*, p. 279, Book Club Associates, 1976.
4   Shakespeare, W., *Measure for Measure*, Act III. Scene 1.16–17.
5   In a television interview with David Frost, 1966.
6   1 Corinthians 15.17, MS.
7   1 Corinthians 15.20.
8   Romans 8.35.
9   Philippians 1.23, MS.

Chapter 24
1   1 Thessalonians 5.9.
2   Lewis, C. S., *The Screwtape Letters*, p. 16, Fontana Books, 1955.
3   Lewis, C. S., *The Screwtape Letters*, p. 60, Fontana Books, 1955.
4   Ephesians 2.8, GNB.
5   1 Corinthians 1.18, GNB.
6   Romans 10.13, MS.
7   1 Thessalonians 5.9.